Reading Skills Competency Tests

ADVANCED LEVEL

Henriette L. Allen, Ph.D.

Henriette L. Allen, Ph.D., is a former classroom teacher in the schools of Coventry, Rhode Island, the Aramco Schools of Dhahran, Saudi Arabia, The American Community School of Benghazi, Libya, and Jackson, Mississippi. Dr. Allen served in several administrative roles, including assistant superintendent of the Jackson Public Schools. She is presently an education consultant recognized nationally. Dr. Allen is the senior author of the series *Competency Tests for Basic Reading Skills* (West Nyack, NY: The Center for Applied Research in Education). She has taught reading skills at both elementary and secondary levels, has supervised the development of a Continuous Progress Reading Program for the Jackson Public Schools, and has lectured widely in the fields of reading, classroom management, technology in the classroom, and leadership in educational administration. Dr. Allen is listed in the *World Who's Who of Women* and *Who's Who—School District Officials*. She was the 1996 recipient of the Distinguished Service Award given by the American Association of School Administrators.

Walter B. Barbe, Ph.D.

A nationally known authority in the fields of reading and learning disabilities, Walter B. Barbe, Ph.D., was for twenty-five years editor-in-chief of the widely acclaimed magazine *Highlights for Children,* and adjunct professor at The Ohio State University. Dr. Barbe is the author of over 150 professional articles and a number of books, including *Personalized Reading Instruction* (West Nyack, NY: Parker Publishing Company, Inc.), coauthored with Jerry L. Abbot. He is also the senior author and editor of two series—*Creative Growth with Handwriting* (Columbus, OH: Zaner-Bloser, Inc.) and *Barbe Reading Skills Check Lists and Activities* (West Nyack, NY: The Center for Applied Research in Education)—and he is senior editor of *Competency Tests for Basic Reading Skills*. Dr. Barbe is a fellow of the American Psychological Association and is listed in *Who's Who in America* and *American Men of Science.*

Brandon B. Sparkman, Ed.D.

Brandon B. Sparkman, Ed.D., is a former assistant superintendent for instruction in the Hartselle, Alabama, City Schools. Dr. Sparkman has worked at all levels of education and is regarded as an authority in the developmental reading skills and early childhood development. He has coauthored several books on preparing preschoolers for school, more specifically, the developmental activities for the reading skills, and has served as a consultant and speaker throughout the nation. He is listed in *Who's Who in America* and *Men of Achievement.*

COMPETENCY TESTS FOR BASIC READING SKILLS
The Center for Applied Research in Education
West Nyack, New York 10994

Library of Congress Cataloging-in-Publication Data

Allen, Henriette L.
    Reading Skills Competency Tests : competency tests for basic
reading skills / Henriette L. Allen, Walter B. Barbe, Brandon B.
Sparkman.
        p.   cm.
    Wiley C. Thornton is named as third author on title pages of v.
2-5.
    Contents: [1] Readiness level — [2] First level — [3] Second
level — [4] Third level — [5] Fourth level — [6] Fifth level —
[7] Sixth level — [8] Advanced level.
    ISBN 0-13-021325-X (v. 1). — ISBN 0-13-021326-8 (v. 2). — ISBN
0-13-021327-6 (v. 3). — ISBN 0-13-021328-4 (v. 4). — ISBN
0-13-021329-2 (v. 5). — ISBN 0-13-021331-4 (v. 6). — ISBN
0-13-021332-2 (v. 7). — ISBN 0-13-021333-0 (v. 8).
    1. Reading Skills Competency Tests.   2. Reading—Ability testing.
I. Barbe, Walter Burke.   II. Sparkman, Brandon B.
III. Title.   IV. Title: Competency tests for basic readingskills.
LB1050.75.R43A45   1999
372.48—dc21   98-51643
                                                          CIP

© 1999 by The Center for Applied Research in Education, West Nyack, NY

Printed in the United States of America

10 9 8 7 6 5 4 3 2 1

ISBN 0-13-021333-0

ATTENTION: CORPORATIONS AND SCHOOLS

The Center for Applied Research in Education books are available at quantity discounts with bulk purchase for educational, business, or sales promotional use. For information, please write to: Prentice Hall Special Sales, 240 Frisch Court, Paramus, NJ 07652. Please supply: title of book, ISBN number, quantity, how the book will be used, date needed.

THE CENTER FOR APPLIED RESEARCH
IN EDUCATION
West Nyack, NY 10994

On the World Wide Web at http://www.phdirect.com

PRENTICE-HALL INTERNATIONAL (UK) LIMITED, *LONDON*
PRENTICE-HALL OF AUSTRALIA PTY. LIMITED, *SYDNEY*
PRENTICE-HALL CANADA INC., *TORONTO*
PRENTICE-HALL HISPANOAMERICANA, S.A., *MEXICO*
PRENTICE-HALL OF INDIA PRIVATE LIMITED, *NEW DELHI*
PRENTICE-HALL OF JAPAN, INC., *TOKYO*
PEARSON EDUCATION ASIA PTE. LTD., *SINGAPORE*
EDITORA PRENTICE-HALL DO BRASIL, LTDA., *RIO DE JANEIRO*

About the *Competency Tests for Basic Reading Skills*

The Reading Skills Competency Tests are a practical tool designed to provide classroom teachers, reading specialists, Title I teachers and others an inventory of those reading skills mastered and those which need to be taught. The tests can be used at all levels with any reading program, as they test mastery of specific reading skills at particular levels.

For easiest use, the test materials are organized into eight distinct units tailored to evaluate children's reading skills at each of the following expectancy and difficulty levels:

Reading Skills Competency Tests: READINESS LEVEL

Reading Skills Competency Tests: FIRST LEVEL

Reading Skills Competency Tests: SECOND LEVEL

Reading Skills Competency Tests: THIRD LEVEL

Reading Skills Competency Tests: FOURTH LEVEL

Reading Skills Competency Tests: FIFTH LEVEL

Reading Skills Competency Tests: SIXTH LEVEL

Reading Skills Competency Tests: ADVANCED LEVEL

The tests give reading teachers a quick, informal means to measure the mastery of reading objectives. They can be used at any time to assess the student's competence in specific reading skills, to pinpoint specific skill weaknesses and problems, and to plan appropriate corrective or remedial instruction in an individualized reading program.

The sequence of the tests corresponds to the sequence of the well-known "Barbe Reading Skills Check Lists," which provide a complete developmental skill sequence from Readiness through Advanced Levels. Each level-unit presents ready-to-use informal tests for evaluating all skills that are listed on the Skills Check List at that level. Tests can be administered individually or to a group by a teacher or a paraprofessional.

Each unit of test materials contains:

1. Directions for using the *Reading Skills Competency Tests* at that grade level to identify individual reading needs and prescribe appropriate instruction.

2. Copies of the Skills Check List and a Group Summary Profile at that grade level for use in individual and group recordkeeping.

3. Reading Skills Competency Tests for assessing all skills at that particular grade level, including teacher test sheets with directions and answer keys for administering and evaluating each test plus reproducible student test sheets.

4. A copy of the "Barbe Reading Skills Sequential Skill Plan" chart.

For easiest use of the materials, complete directions are provided in each unit for using the Competency Tests at that level and for recording the information on the student skills Check List and the Group Summary Profile.

The test items in each level-unit correspond to the skills indicated on the Check List. The Check List can be marked to indicate which skills the child has mastered or the skills in which further instruction is needed. The Group Summary Profile can be used to obtain an overall picture of class progress and to identify the skills which need to be taught. It is also useful in identifying small groups with similar needs, students who require personalized help on a prerequisite skill, and students who need continued help on a current skill.

You will find that these tests provide for:

- quick, informal assessment of students' competence in reading skills
- diagnosis and prescription of specific reading skill weaknesses and needs
- devising of appropriate teaching strategies for individuals and small or large groups
- continuous evaluation of each child's progress in the basic reading skills
- flexibility in planning the reading instructional program
- immediate feedback to the student and the teacher

The Competency Tests for Basic Reading Skills can be used by all reading teachers in either a self-contained classroom or a team setting. They are as flexible as the teacher chooses to make them. Hopefully, they will provide an efficient, systematic means to identify the specific reading skills that students need to learn and thus meet, to a greater degree, their individual reading needs.

Henriette L. Allen

Walter B. Barbe

Contents

How to Use the Competency Tests and Check List

A major task for teachers is verifying mastery of basic skills and keeping records. Recordkeeping and competency tests are of greater concern today than ever before. But knowing of their necessity does not make the task any easier. Competency tests and the accompanying records may be compared to a road map. One must drive through Town B to reach Town W. Competency tests are designed to assist you in verifying mastery of basic reading skills, and to indicate where to begin on the journey of reading mastery. The Reading Skills Check Lists provide check points to verify (1) where the student is on the sequence of skills, (2) when the skills were mastered, and (3) at what rate he or she is progressing.

In order for skills to develop sequentially, it is vital that we have an idea of where a student is within the sequence of reading skills. The Reading Skills Competency Tests and Check List in this unit are designed to help you teach directly to identified student needs, on a day-to-day, week-to-week, and month-to-month basis.

The Reading Skills Competency Tests are easy-to-administer tests for each reading skill on the "Barbe Reading Skills Check Lists." Directions for administering each test are given on a teacher page. This page also provides the answer key and the number of correct responses needed for mastery. Facing the teacher page is the student test page, which can be used as a master for copying when reproduction for classroom use is via copy machine.

The Check Lists are not intended as a rigid program for reading instruction. Rather they are meant to provide a general pattern around which a program may be built. The Advanced Level Skills Check List is divided into two parts. Part One has four headings: Vocabulary, Word Attack Skills, Comprehension, and Oral and Silent Reading. Part Two also has four major headings: Vocabulary, Comprehension, Study Skills, and Creative Reading. Each area is of great importance to the student's development. In presenting the skills on the Check List, it is recommended that you deal alternately with some activities from each of the four major headings.

You will find a copy of the Advanced Level Skills Check List on pages 14 and 15, which you can copy and use for individual recordkeeping.

Begin at the Beginning

Before planning an instructional program for any pupil, it is necessary to determine at what level the student is reading. This may be determined through the use of an informal reading inventory. It is then necessary to identify which basic reading skills the pupil has mastered and which skills need remediation or initial teaching.

The Reading Skills Competency Tests offer a quick, practical means to determine which skills the student has mastered and on which the student needs additional work. It is suggested that the tests be administered at the beginning of a school year. The tests may also be used at any time throughout the year to determine a student's entry point in a Reading Skills Class, or to reevaluate the progress of individual students. The tests may be given to a large group, a small group, or an individual, whichever is appropriate for those being tested and for the test being administered. Some tests, such as Oral Reading, must be administered individually. The entry point into the reading program should be at that point when a student begins to encounter difficulty with a particular reading skill.

The tests may be used as a pre test to indicate where instruction is needed, and the same tests may also be used as a post test to indicate mastery or non-mastery. Once a pupil's areas of difficulty are identified, you may then plan instructional activities accordingly. After the student has worked through a unit of instruction, you may use the same test to verify mastery of the skill. When mastery occurs, the student is advanced to another skill. When the student is unsuccessful on the specific test item, additional instruction is needed. If a reasonable amount of instruction does not result in mastery, it may be that changing instructional approaches is needed or that more work is needed on earlier skills.

Once you have decided the level of mastery tests needed, the assessing part of the reading program is ready to begin. Specific directions are given for each test. At the Advanced Level, you may assign the test to be taken and permit the student to work independently. The directions are given at the top of every student test page. In some instances, as in oral reading, you may have to test each student individually.

Recording on the Check List

Recordkeeping is an important part in any instructional design. Simplicity and ease is vital. One effective method for marking a Skills Check List is as follows:

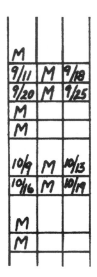

II. Word Attack Skills
    A. Knows consonant sounds
        1.   Initial single consonants of one sound
        2.   Sounds of C and G
        3.   Blends ___ digraph ___ diphthong ___
        4.   Medial sounds
        5.   Final sounds
    B. Hears and can make vowel sounds
        1.   Long vowels ___ short vowels ___
        2.   Can apply vowel rules
    C. Knows elements of syllabication
        1.   Knows rules
        2.   Can apply rules

Put an M in the first column if the pupil takes a test and demonstrates mastery of that basic reading skill. If the pupil has not mastered the skill, record the date. The date in column one indicates when instruction in the skill began. When the pupil is tested a second time, put an M in the second column if mastery is achieved, and record the date of mastery in the third column. Thus, anyone looking at the Check List can tell if the student mastered the skill before instruction or when instruction began, and when the skill was actually mastered. The Check List provides a written record of: (1) where the student is on the sequence of reading skills, (2) when the student mastered the skills, and (3) at what rate the student is progressing.

Conferencing with the Pupil

The student and teacher may discuss performance on the Competency Tests and Check List and jointly plan subsequent instruction. The Check List provides a guide for this discussion.

Conferencing with Parents

The Reading Skills Check List also serves as a guide for parent conferences. Using the Check List you can talk with parents about specific skills mastered, as well as those which have been taught but not yet fully mastered. Use of the Check List reassures parents of your concern for skill instruction, your knowledge of ways to aid their child in becoming a better reader, and of your professional plan which considers each child individually.

Conferencing with Professional Staff

Conferences with other staff such as school psychologists, counselors, and principals concerning an individual child's reading progress should focus on the instructional plan. When Check Lists are used, other professional staff members are provided with a written record of the teacher's progress and the child's progress in this program. The Check List provides information on the skills mastered, and when the skills were mastered.

Providing Check Lists to the Next Grade Level Teacher

One of the great problems in teaching reading skills at the beginning of the year is to know where to begin. If the Reading Skills Check Lists are passed along from class to class, the new teacher will know the skill level of every student in the room.

Making a Group Summary Profile from Individual Check Lists

While the Reading Skills Check List is intended primarily for individual use, there are various reasons for bringing together a record of the instructional needs of the entire class. In planning classroom strategies, you will find the use of the Group Profile on pages 18 to 20 helpful.

After you have recorded the skill level for each student on the Reading Skills Check List, you may then enter this information on the Group Profile. The Group Summary Profile is designed to help you identify groups of students who need a particular skill. It is a visual representation of the instructional needs of the entire class. It also presents the specific strengths and achievement levels of individual students.

The Group Profile may be used in conferences with supervisors and administrators to discuss the status of a particular class, the point of initial instruction, and the progress made to date. A different colored pen or pencil may be used to indicate the different grading or marking periods of the school year. This further indicates the progress the pupils have made within these periods of time.

The Group Profile can indicate the instructional materials and supplies which are needed. Since specific reading skills needs will be clearly identified, materials may be purchased which meet these needs.

Ensuring the Sequential Presentation of Skills

One of the goals of reading instruction is to develop a love of reading. But if students are to develop a love of reading, they must be able to read with efficiency. And in order to be efficient readers they must have at their ready command all of the necessary skills, including the ability to unlock new words and to read rapidly.

If the skills are to be mastered, they must be presented sequentially. When skills are presented out of sequence, critical skills are in danger of being bypassed or given minimal attention.

In many instances, the sequence of skills is firmly established; in other instances the sequence is less rigid. In these Check Lists, the skills have been placed in the order the authors feel is logical. Teachers should be free to change this sequence when there is reason to do so, being careful not to eliminate the presentation of the skill.

It is important that some skill instruction be conducted in groups. This prevents individual students from becoming isolated, a danger which sometimes occurs when too much individualization is undertaken.

Using the Sequential Skill Plan Chart

The importance of viewing the total sequential skills program cannot be minimized. The chart is intended primarily for use by the classroom teacher. If a personalized approach is used in teaching reading skills, it is still essential that the teacher view the skills as a continuous progression rather than as skills for a specific grade level. This chart allows the teacher to view not only those skills that are taught principally at the present grade placement, but also those skills which will be taught as the student progresses.

As an inservice tool, the chart provides teachers with the opportunity to see their own positions in the skills progression. It should be understood, of course, that there are any number of reasons why decisions may be made to teach the skills at levels different from those indicated on the chart. But it is important that reading skills be taught, and that basically they be taught in a sequential manner, in a planned reading program. Incidental teaching of reading skills often results in vital skills being neglected, or being bypassed until the student encounters difficulties. At that point, having to go back to earlier skills is more difficult and less effective.

The chart also provides administrators, supervisors, and teachers with direction for a total skills program.

Reading Skills Check List— Advanced Level

On the following pages you will find a copy of the "Barbe Reading Skills Check List— Advanced Level." The Check List presents a sequential outline of the skills to be mastered at this level in six major areas: Vocabulary, Word Attack Skills, Comprehension, Oral and Silent Reading, Study Skills, and Creative Reading.

You may photocopy the Advanced Level Check List as many times as you need it for use in individual recordkeeping.

Accompanying the unit is a copy of the "Barbe Reading Skills Check List Sequential Skill Plan." This chart provides a visual representation of the total reading skills progression through all levels, including:

Readiness Level

First Level

Second Level

Third Level

Fourth Level

Fifth Level

Sixth Level

Advanced Level

BARBE READING SKILLS CHECK LIST
ADVANCED LEVEL

(Last Name)   (First Name)   (Name of School)

(Age)   (Grade Placement)   (Name of Teacher)

PART ONE

I. Vocabulary:

A. Word Recognition in Content:
- English ____
- Mathematics ____
- Social Studies ____
- Science ____

B. Identifies Compound Words

C. Root Words
1. Recognizes and understands concept of root words
2. Knows meaning of common roots

D. Prefixes
1. Recognizes and knows concept of prefixes
2. Knows meaning of common prefixes:

anti-	against	antibiotic
co-	together with	cooperate
de-	down, from, away	deploy
dis-	apart from, reversing	dismantle
en-	in	encourage
ex-	out of, beyond	extrovert
pre-	before	preview
pro-	for, forward	propeller
un-	not	unkind

E. Suffixes
1. Recognizes and knows concept of suffixes
2. Knows meaning of common suffixes:

ary	place where	primary
ist	one who acts	scientist
ive	relating to	constructive
less	without	fearless
ly	similar in manner	definitely
ment	state, quality, act	contentment
ness	state of being	happiness
ous	abounding in	righteous
hood	condition of	statehood

F. Knows meaning of terms in vocabulary of language:
1. simile ____ metaphor ____
2. synonyms ____ antonyms ____ homonyms ____
3. onomatopoeia ____

II. Word Attack Skills:

A. Knows consonant sounds
1. Initial single consonants of one sound
2. Sounds of **c** and **g**
3. Blends ____ digraph ____ diphthong ____
4. Medial sounds
5. Final sounds

B. Hears and can make vowel sounds
1. Long vowels ____ short vowels ____
2. Can apply vowel rules

C. Knows elements of syllabication
1. Knows rules
2. Can apply rules

D. Uses accent properly
1. Knows and applies rules
2. Can shift accent and change use of word

III. Comprehension:

A. Understands structure of story or paragraph:
- main idea
- topic sentence
- sequence of ideas
- subordinate ideas

B. Can repeat general idea of material read

C. Can remember specific important facts

D. Can relate material read to known information or experience

E. Can follow printed directions

F. Can interpret hidden meaning

IV. Silent and Oral Reading:

A. Reads silently without lip movements

B. Reads silently at twice oral rate

C. Adjusts silent rate to material
1. Reads popular fiction at 200+ words per minute
2. Uses skimming techniques when applicable

D. Eye-voice span 3 to 5 words (in oral reading)

E. Reads aloud with comprehension

PART TWO—Advanced Level

I. Vocabulary:

A. Increases vocabulary through wide reading
B. Organizes own word-study techniques
II. Comprehension:
A. Interpretation
   1. Sequences events from multiple sources
   2. Makes generalizations from multiple sources
   3. Identifies relationships of elements from multiple sources
   4. Identifies author's purpose
   5. Develops use of parts of speech through transformation of sentences

B. Application
   1. Uses multiple sources for documentation and support for opinion
   2. Uses maps, graphs, charts, tables when appropriate in response to readings
   3. Takes notes during debate and other presentations in order to summarize and respond to logic used
   4. Uses reading for different purposes:
      a. practical information
      b. problem solving
      c. recreation

C. Analysis
   1. Differentiates between types of sentences:
      a. expository
      b. narrative
      c. descriptive
      d. persuasive

D. Synthesis
   1. Extends generalizations beyond sources
   2. Hypothesizes
   3. Suggests alternatives and opinions

E. Critical Evaluation
   1. Develops own criteria for critical review of materials:
      a. fiction
      b. propaganda
      c. nonfiction

      d. essays
      e. journals
      f. biographies
   2. Makes judgments about author's qualifications
   3. Judges reasonableness between statements and conclusions
III. Study Skills:
A. Uses thesaurus, almanac, atlas, maps and globes

B. Uses variety of media to complete assignments and purposes

C. Uses outlining and note-taking skills

D. Adjusts reading speed to material and purpose
E. Demonstrates independence in locating, selecting and using materials to own purpose

F. Applies problem solving approach: identifies problem, gathers information, devises possible solutions, selects option, uses option, evaluates

G. Designs, uses and revises own study schedules

H. Locates sources within a book by using table of contents and index

IV. Creative Reading:

A. Recognizes figurative language, dialect and colloquial speech

B. Recognizes literary forms:
   1. folk literature: tables, songs, fables, legends and myths
   2. short story
   3. nonfiction including propaganda
   4. poetry, limerick, couplet, sonnet, blank verse and internal rhyme

C. Compares value systems of characters

D. Understands settings: social, economic, and educational

E. Responds to the author's background
F. Responds to the author's style of mood and point-of-view

Group Summary Profile— Advanced Level

The following pages present a Group Summary Profile at the Advanced Level which you can use to record the progress of the entire class in mastering the specific reading skills at that level. This profile can assist you in identifying groups of students who need instruction in a particular skill as well as in assessing the strengths and achievement levels of individual students. The Group Profile may also be used in conferences with administrators to discuss the status of a particular class.

Name of Teacher: _____

GROUP SUMMARY
PROFILE
ADVANCED LEVEL

Student Names

	I. Vocabulary:	A. Word Recognition in Content	B. Identifies Compound Words	C. Root Words	1. Recognizes and understands concept of root words	2. Knows meaning of common roots	D. Prefixes	1. Recognizes and understands concept of prefixes	2. Knows meaning of common prefixes	E. Suffixes	1. Recognizes and understands concept of suffixes	2. Knows meaning of common suffixes	F. Knows meaning of terms in vocabulary	1. simile metaphor	2. synonyms antonyms homonyms	3. onomatopoeia	II. Word Attack Skills:	A. Knows consonant sounds	1. Initial single consonants of one sound	2. Sounds of c and g	3. Blends digraph diphthong	4. Medial sounds	5. Final sounds	B. Hears and can make vowel sounds	1. Long vowels short vowels

(PART ONE)

School: _____ Year:

2. Can apply vowel rules
C. Knows elements of syllabication
1. Know rules
2. Can apply rules
D. Uses accent properly
1. Knows and applies rules
2. Can shift accent and change use of word
III. Comprehension:
A. Understands structure of story or paragraph
   main idea topic sentence sequence of ideas
   subordinate ideas
B. Can repeat general idea of material read
C. Can remember specific important facts
D. Can relate material read to know information
E. Can follow printed directions
F. Can interpret hidden meaning
IV. Silent and Oral Reading:
A. Reads silently without lip movements
B. Reads silently at twice oral rate
C. Adjust silent rate to material
1. Reads popular fiction at 200+ words per minute
2. Uses skimming techniques when applicable
D. Eye-voice span 3 to 5 words (in oral reading)
E. Reads aloud with comprehension
I. Vocabulary:
A. Increases vocabulary through wide reading
B. Organizes own word study techniques
II. Comprehension:
A. Interpretation
1. Sequences events from multiple sources
2. Makes generalizations from multiple sources
3. Identifies relationships of elements from multiple
   sources
4. Identifies author's purpose
5. Develops use of parts of speech
B. Application
1. Uses multiple sources for documentation
2. Uses maps, graphs, charts, tables

PART TWO

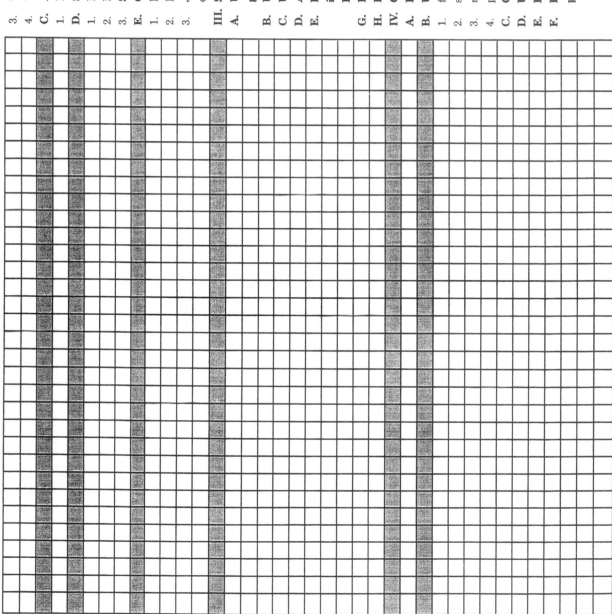

3. Takes notes to summarize and respond
4. Uses reading for different purposes
C. **Analysis**
1. Differentiates between types of sentences
D. **Synthesis**
1. Extends generalizations beyond sources
2. Hypothesizes
3. Suggests alternatives and options
E. **Critical Evaluation**
1. Develops own criteria for critical review
2. Makes judgments about author's qualifications
3. Judges reasonableness between statements and conclusions
III. **Study Skills:**
A. Uses thesaurus, almanac, atlas, maps, and globes
B. Uses variety of media
C. Uses outlining and note-taking skills
D. Adjusts reading speed to material and purpose
E. Demonstrates independence in locating, selecting and using materials to own purpose
F. Applies problem solving approach
G. Designs, uses and revises own study schedules
H. Locates sources within a book
IV. **Creative Reading:**
A. Recognizes figurative language
B. Understands literary forms:
1. folk literature
2. short story
3. nonfiction including propaganda
4. poetry, limerick, couplet, sonnet, blank verse
C. Compares value systems of characters
D. Understands settings
E. Responds to the author's background
F. Responds to the author's style of mood and point-of-view

Reading Skills Competency Tests Advanced Level

Henriette L. Allen, Ph.D.
Brandon B. Sparkman, Ed.D.

The test items which follow are written to measure the reading skills on the "Barbe Reading Skills Check List—Advanced Level."

The Competency Tests and Check List provide for:

- a quick, informal assessment of a student's competence in reading skills
- diagnosis and prescription of specific reading skill weaknesses and needs
- devising of appropriate teaching strategies for individuals and small or large groups
- continuous evaluation of each student's progress in the basic reading skills
- flexibility in planning the reading instructional program
- immediate feedback to the student and the teacher

The tests are designed to give you an efficient, systematic means to identify the specific reading skills needs of students.

ADVANCED LEVEL—Part One

I. VOCABULARY A. Word Recognition in Content

OBJECTIVE: The student will demonstrate the ability to recognize vocabulary words in English, mathematics, social studies, and science content.

DIRECTIONS: Many words relate to more than one subject area according to the way they are used or the context in which they are used. Study the sentences below. There is one underlined word in each sentence. Indicate the subject content in which the word is used by placing the appropriate numeral in the space provided.

1. English 2. mathematics 3. social studies 4. science

_3_ 1. The professor enjoyed his experiment dealing with the reactions of city and rural dwellers to political positions of candidates.

_4_ 2. The professor enjoyed his experiment dealing with the chemical reactions of certain acids when mixed with H_2O.

_3_ 3. Expansion of territory was the motive of aggressive nations during the eighteenth century.

_2_ 4. Expansion of numbers is carefully explained in the chapter dealing with "expanded notation."

_1_ 5. As he composed the letter he made certain that the body contained no errors.

_4_ 6. The composition of the body was carefully studied in the laboratory.

_1_ 7. Knowledge of the Dewey Decimal System is critical to finding good reading material.

_2_ 8. The decimal system must be understood before one can become a proficient shopper.

MASTERY REQUIREMENT: 7 correct responses

Indicate mastery on the student response sheet with a check.

ADVANCED LEVEL—Part One

I. VOCABULARY

A. Word Recognition in Content

Name _____

Date _____

Mastery _____

DIRECTIONS: Many words relate to more than one subject area according to the way they are used or the context in which they are used. Study the sentences below. There is one underlined word in each sentence. Indicate the subject content in which the word is used by placing the appropriate numeral in the space provided.

1. English   2. mathematics   3. social studies   4. science

_____ 1. The professor enjoyed his experiment dealing with the reactions of city and rural dwellers to political positions of candidates.

_____ 2. The professor enjoyed his experiment dealing with the chemical reactions of certain acids when mixed with H_2O.

_____ 3. Expansion of territory was the motive of aggressive nations during the eighteenth century.

_____ 4. Expansion of numbers is carefully explained in the chapter dealing with "expanded notation."

_____ 5. As he composed the letter he made certain that the body contained no errors.

_____ 6. The composition of the body was carefully studied in the laboratory.

_____ 7. Knowledge of the Dewey Decimal System is critical to finding good reading material.

_____ 8. The decimal system must be understood before one can become a proficient shopper.

I. VOCABULARY   B. Identifies Compound Words

OBJECTIVE: The student will identify compound words.

DIRECTIONS: Place a check (√) by each compound word.

    ____   1. peaceful

    ____   2. misspell

    √   3. drumstick

    √   4. eyesore

    ____   5. lastly

    √   6. battleship

    √   7. spearhead

    √   8. toothache

    ____   9. unkind

    √   10. flashlight

MASTERY REQUIREMENT: 8 correct responses

Indicate mastery on the student response sheet with a check.

ADVANCED LEVEL—Part One

I. VOCABULARY

B. Identifies Compound Words

Name _____

Date _____

Mastery _____

DIRECTIONS: Place a check (√) by each compound word.

_____ 1. peaceful

_____ 2. misspell

_____ 3. drumstick

_____ 4. eyesore

_____ 5. lastly

_____ 6. battleship

_____ 7. spearhead

_____ 8. toothache

_____ 9. unkind

_____ 10. flashlight

I. VOCABULARY   C. Root Words   1. Recognizes and understands concept of root words

OBJECTIVE: The pupil will demonstrate that he/she recognizes and understands the concept of root words.

DIRECTIONS: Read the following words; then underline the root word in each word.

1. un<u>kind</u>ness

2. <u>slow</u>ly

3. over<u>shoot</u>

4. pre<u>fix</u>

5. out<u>law</u>

6. out<u>distance</u>

7. under<u>rate</u>

8. un<u>just</u>ly

9. law<u>man</u>

10. <u>right</u>fully

MASTERY REQUIREMENT: 8 correct responses

Indicate mastery on the student response sheet with a check.

I. VOCABULARY

Name _____

C. Root Words

Date _____

    1. Recognizes and
        understands concept
        of root words

Mastery _____

DIRECTIONS: Read the following words; then underline the root word in each word.

1. unkindness

2. slowly

3. overshoot

4. prefix

5. outlaw

6. outdistance

7. underrate

8. unjustly

9. lawman

10. rightfully

I.   VOCABULARY   C.   Root Words   2.   Knows meaning of common root words

OBJECTIVE: The student will demonstrate that he/she knows the meaning of common root words.

DIRECTIONS: The words in the left column are root words. The words in the right column are the meanings of the root words. Match the correct meaning to each root word by writing the letter found beside the meaning on the line to the left of the root word.

	Root words		*Meaning*
j	1. graph	a.	sound
a	2. phon	b.	sleep
g	3. hydr	c.	say
d	4. therm	d.	heat
i	5. meter	e.	walk
c	6. dic	f.	throw
e	7. ambul	g.	water
b	8. dorm	h.	hear
h	9. audi	i.	measure
f	10. ject	j.	writing

MASTERY REQUIREMENT: 8 correct responses

Indicate mastery on the student response sheet with a check.

I.   VOCABULARY

Name _____

C.   Root Words

Date _____

2.   **Knows meaning of common root words**

Mastery _____

DIRECTIONS: The words in the left column are root words. The words in the right column are the meanings of the root words. Match the correct meaning to each root word by writing the letter found beside the meaning on the line to the left of the root word.

Root words   *Meanings*

_____   1. graph   a.   sound

_____   2. phon   b.   sleep

_____   3. hydr   c.   say

_____   4. therm   d.   heat

_____   5. meter   e.   walk

_____   6. dic   f.   throw

_____   7. ambul   g.   water

_____   8. dorm   h.   hear

_____   9. audi   i.   measure

_____ 10. ject   j.   writing

I. VOCABULARY   D. Prefixes   1. Recognizes and knows concept of prefixes

OBJECTIVE: The student will recognize and know the concept of prefixes.

DIRECTIONS: If the words listed below have a prefix, underline the part that is a prefix.

1. listless

2. <u>pre</u>view

3. audition

4. <u>in</u>visible

5. <u>mis</u>spelled

6. regardless

7. blindness

8. <u>fore</u>tell

9. <u>under</u>bid

10. lastly

MASTERY REQUIREMENT: 8 correct responses

Indicate mastery on the student response sheet with a check.

ADVANCED LEVEL—Part One

I. VOCABULARY

Name _____

D. Prefixes

1. Recognizes and knows
   concept of prefixes

Date _____

Mastery _____

DIRECTIONS: If the words listed below have a prefix, underline the part that is a prefix.

1. listless

2. preview

3. audition

4. invisible

5. misspelled

6. regardless

7. blindness

8. foretell

9. underbid

10. lastly

I. VOCABULARY   D. Prefixes   2. Knows meaning of common prefixes

OBJECTIVE: The student will demonstrate knowledge of the meaning of common prefixes.

DIRECTIONS: The prefixes are in the left column. The words in the right column tell what the prefixes mean. Match the correct meaning to each prefix by writing the letter found beside the meaning in the space provided by the prefix.

	Prefixes		*Meanings*
c	1. anti-	a.	down, from, away
e	2. co-	b.	in
a	3. de-	c.	against
i	4. dis-	d.	before
b	5. en-	e.	together with
h	6. ex-	f.	for, forward
d	7. pre-	g.	not
f	8. pro-	h.	out of, beyond
g	9. un-	i.	apart from, reversing

MASTERY REQUIREMENT: 7 correct responses

Indicate mastery on the student response sheet with a check.

ADVANCED LEVEL—Part One

I. VOCABULARY

Name _____

  D. Prefixes

  2. Knows meaning of
      common prefixes

Date _____

Mastery _____

DIRECTIONS: The prefixes are in the left column. The words in the right column tell what the prefixes mean. Match the correct meaning to each prefix by writing the letter found beside the meaning in the space provided by the prefix.

Prefixes	*Meanings*
____ 1. anti-	a. down, from, away
____ 2. co-	b. in
____ 3. de-	c. against
____ 4. dis-	d. before
____ 5. en-	e. together with
____ 6. ex-	f. for, forward
____ 7. pre-	g. not
____ 8. pro-	h. out of, beyond
____ 9. un-	i. apart from, reversing

ADVANCED LEVEL—Part One

I. VOCABULARY   E. Suffixes   1. Recognizes and knows concept of suffixes

OBJECTIVE: The student will demonstrate that he/she recognizes and knows the concept of suffixes.

DIRECTIONS: Underline the suffix when found in words listed below.

    1. list<u>less</u>

    2. uncover

    3. previe<u>er</u>

    4. sense<u>less</u>

    5. construct<u>ive</u>

    6. opera<u>tion</u>

    7. consume

    8. man<u>hood</u>

    9. slow<u>ly</u>

   10. beaut<u>iful</u>

MASTERY REQUIREMENT: 9 correct responses

Indicate mastery on the student response sheet with a check.

ADVANCED LEVEL—Part One

I. VOCABULARY

Name _____

E. Suffixes

1. Recognizes and knows
   concept of suffixes

Date _____

Mastery _____

DIRECTIONS: Underline the suffix when found in words listed below.

1. listless

2. uncover

3. previewer

4. senseless

5. constructive

6. operation

7. consume

8. manhood

9. slowly

10. beautiful

ADVANCED LEVEL—Part One

I. VOCABULARY   E.   Suffixes   2.   Knows meaning of common suffixes

OBJECTIVES: The student will demonstrate knowledge of the meaning of common suffixes.

DIRECTIONS: The suffixes are in the left column. In the right column are words that tell what the suffixes mean. Match the correct meaning to each suffix by writing the letter found beside the meaning in the space provided by the suffix.

Suffixes			*Meanings*	
__d__	1.	ary (literary)	a.	one who acts
__a__	2.	ist (pianist)	b.	state of being
__g__	3.	ive (active)	c.	without
__c__	4.	less (regardless)	d.	place where
__e__	5.	ly (hurriedly)	e.	similar in manner
__i__	6.	ment (achievement)	f.	condition of
__b__	7.	ness (fullness)	g.	relating to
__h__	8.	ous (joyous)	h.	abounding in
__f__	9.	hood (childhood)	i.	state, quality, act

MASTERY REQUIREMENT: 6 correct responses

Indicate mastery on the student response sheet with a check.

ADVANCED LEVEL—Part One

I. **VOCABULARY**

   E. **Suffixes**

      2. **Knows meaning of common suffixes**

Name _____

Date _____

Mastery _____

DIRECTIONS: The suffixes are in the left column. In the right column are words that tell what the suffixes mean. Match the correct meaning to each suffix by writing the letter found beside the meaning in the space provided by the suffix.

Suffixes			*Meanings*	
____	1.	ary (literary)	a.	one who acts
____	2.	ist (pianist)	b.	state of being
____	3.	ive (active)	c.	without
____	4.	less (regardless)	d.	place where
____	5.	ly (hurriediy)	e.	similar in manner
____	6.	ment (achievement)	f.	condition of
____	7.	ness (fullness)	g.	relating to
____	8.	ous (joyous)	h.	abounding in
____	9.	hood (childhood)	i.	state, quality, act

I. VOCABULARY   F. Knows Meaning of Terms in Vocabulary of Language:
Simile, Metaphor, Synonyms, Antonyms, Homonyms,
Onomatopoeia

OBJECTIVE: The student will know the meaning of simile, metaphor, synonyms, antonyms, homonyms, and onomatopoeia.

DIRECTIONS: Match the vocabulary terms listed below with their definitions by writing the letter found beside the term in the space provided by the correct definition.

a. simile   d. antonyms

b. metaphor   e. homonyms

c. synonyms   f. onomatopoeia

_f_ 1. Formation of a word by imitating the natural sound associated with the object or action involved   (buzz–tinkle)

_d_ 2. Words of opposite meaning   (soft–hard)

_a_ 3. A figure of speech in which one thing is likened to another dissimilar thing by the use of like, as, etc.   (eyes like stars)

_e_ 4. Words that are pronounced alike but have different meaning and usually different spelling   (hole–whole)

_b_ 5. A figure of speech in which words that ordinarily mean one thing are applied to something else to suggest a common quality   (nerves of steel)

_c_ 6. Words of similar meaning   (mourn–grieve)

MASTERY REQUIREMENT: 6 correct responses

Indicate mastery on the student response sheet with a check.

I. **VOCABULARY**

Name _____

   F. **Knows Meaning of Terms**
      in Vocabulary of Language:
      Simile, Metaphor, Synonyms,
      Antonyms, Homonyms,
      Onomatopoeia

Date _____

Mastery _____

DIRECTIONS: Match the vocabulary terms listed below with their definitions by writing the letter found beside the term in the space provided by the correct definition.

     a. simile   d. antonyms

     b. metaphor   e. homonyms

     c. synonyms   f. onomatopoeia

_____ 1. Formation of a word by imitating the natural sound associated with the object or action involved (buzz—tinkle)

_____ 2. Words of opposite meaning (soft—hard)

_____ 3. A figure of speech in which one thing is likened to another dissimilar thing by the use of like, as, etc. (eyes like stars)

_____ 4. Words that are pronounced alike but have different meaning and usually different spelling (hole—whole)

_____ 5. A figure of speech in which words that ordinarily mean one thing are applied to something else to suggest a common quality (nerves of steel)

_____ 6. Words of similar meaning (mourn—grieve)

ADVANCED LEVEL—Part One

I. VOCABULARY   F.   Knows Meaning of Terms in Vocabulary of Language

                    1.   Simile, Metaphor

OBJECTIVE: The student will demonstrate a knowledge of similes and metaphors.

DIRECTIONS: Read the following sentences carefully. Underline the simile or metaphor. At the beginning of the sentence, write an "S" if the underlined phrase is a simile and an "M" if the underlined phrase is a metaphor.

__S__   1. The poet wrote the overused line ". . . and her cheeks like rosebuds."

__M__   2. The vampire's hands of ice circled the damsel's throat and slowly tightened.

__M__   3. As the will was being read, her stepmother's dagger eyes pierced Cinderella.

__M__   4. The baby's rose-petal skin was a delight to touch.

__S__   5. She was described as having a heart as hard as steel.

__S__   6. Eddie ran for third base as speedy as a rabbit.

__S__   7. Janet entered the room and walked about as stately as a queen.

__S__   8. Buster's kingly deportment was considered as becoming as a rainbow to a shower.

__M__   9. Vinegar sharp words and eerie sounds were heard coming from the witches' convention.

__M__   10. The clown's gunboat shoes flapped about as he strutted in the center ring.

MASTERY REQUIREMENT: 8 correct responses

Indicate mastery on the student response sheet with a check.

I. VOCABULARY

Name _____

F. Knows Meaning of
   Terms in Vocabulary
   of Language

Date _____

1. Simile, Metaphor

Mastery _____

DIRECTIONS: Read the following sentences carefully. Underline the simile or metaphor. At the beginning of the sentence, write an "S" if the underlined phrase is a simile and an "M" if the underlined phrase is a metaphor.

_____ 1. The poet wrote the overused line "... and her cheeks like rosebuds."

_____ 2. The vampire's hands of ice circled the damsel's throat and slowly tightened.

_____ 3. As the will was being read, her stepmother's dagger eyes pierced Cinderella.

_____ 4. The baby's rose-petal skin was a delight to touch.

_____ 5. She was described as having a heart as hard as steel.

_____ 6. Eddie ran for third base as speedy as a rabbit.

_____ 7. Janet entered the room and walked about as stately as a queen.

_____ 8. Buster's kingly deportment was considered as becoming as a rainbow to a shower.

_____ 9. Vinegar sharp words and eerie sounds were heard coming from the witches' convention.

_____ 10. The clown's gunboat shoes flapped about as he strutted in the center ring.

ADVANCED LEVEL—Part One

I. VOCABULARY   F.   Knows Meaning of Terms in Vocabulary of Language

2.   Antonyms, Homonyms, Synonyms

OBJECTIVE: The student will demonstrate an understanding of the terms antonyms, synonyms and homonyms.

DIRECTIONS: Read the following groups of words. On the line next to the words write "S" for synonyms, "A" for antonyms, and "H" for homonyms.

__A__   1.   enemy—friend

__H__   2.   bare—bear

__S__   3.   task—assignment

__S__   4.   caring—comforting

__H__   5.   sew—so

__A__   6.   war—peace

__S__   7.   trouble—problem

__H__   8.   hi—high

__A__   9.   scold-praise

__A__   10.   float—sink

__S__   11.   respond—answer

__H__   12.   some—sum

MASTERY REQUIREMENT: 10 correct responses

Indicate mastery on the student response sheet with a check.

ADVANCED LEVEL—Part One

I. VOCABULARY   Name _____

    F. Knows Meaning of
        Terms in Vocabulary   Date _____
        of Language

        2. Antonyms, Homonyms,   Mastery _____
            Synonyms

DIRECTIONS: Read the following groups of words. On the line next to the words write "S"
             for synonyms, "A" for antonyms, and "H" for homonyms.

        _____   1. enemy—friend

        _____   2. bare—bear

        _____   3. task—assignment

        _____   4. caring—comforting

        _____   5. sew—so

        _____   6. war—peace

        _____   7. trouble—problem

        _____   8. hi—high

        _____   9. scold—praise

        _____ 10. float—sink

        _____ 11. respond—answer

        _____ 12. some—sum

I. VOCABULARY   F. **Knows Meaning of Terms in Vocabulary of Language**

3. Onomatopoeia

OBJECTIVE: The student will demonstrate an understanding of onomatopoeia.

DIRECTIONS: Underline the onomatopoetic expression(s) in the following sentences.

1. The boys listened to the buzzing of the bees and the chirping of the birds.

2. The buzzing alarm was quickly shut off.

3. The oven's timer rang for several seconds.

4. The whirring of the lawn mowers was distracting to the students.

5. The washing machine's whirring sound was a delight to the repairman after four hours of tedious labor.

6. The humming hair dryers drowned out the girls' conversation.

7. The doorbell's chimes were a delight to hear.

8. The purring engines roared as the signal went down for the race to begin.

9. The electric mixer went chugging along like a broken-down mule train.

10. The sleek new automobile's engine went from gear to gear without screeching.

MASTERY REQUIREMENT: 8 correct responses

Indicate mastery on the student response sheet with a check.

ADVANCED LEVEL–Part One

I. **VOCABULARY**

    F. **Knows Meaning of**
       Terms in Vocabulary
       of Language

       3. **Onomatopoeia**

Name _____

Date _____

Mastery _____

DIRECTIONS: Underline the onomatopoetic expression(s) in the following sentences.

1. The boys listened to the buzzing of the bees and the chirping of the birds.

2. The buzzing alarm was quickly shut off.

3. The oven's timer rang for several seconds.

4. The whirring of the lawn mowers was distracting to the students.

5. The washing machine's whirring sound was a delight to the repairman after four hours of tedious labor.

6. The humming hair dryers drowned out the girls' conversation.

7. The doorbell's chimes were a delight to hear.

8. The purring engines roared as the signal went down for the race to begin.

9. The electric mixer went chugging along like a broken-down mule train.

10. The sleek new automobile's engine went from gear to gear without screeching.

© 1999 by The Center for Applied Research in Education, Inc.

ADVANCED LEVEL—Part One

II. WORD ATTACK SKILLS   A.   Knows Consonant Sounds   1.   Initial single consonants of one sound
4.   Medial sounds
5.   Final sounds

OBJECTIVE: The student will demonstrate a knowledge of the sounds of initial single consonants of one sound, medial consonant sounds, and final consonant sounds.

DIRECTIONS: The consonants shown in the left column are used in the initial, middle, and final positions in the words on the same line. Underline the designated consonant in each word, then write its sound in the space provided.

Example: g   _g_   young   _j_   gem   _j_   age

          b   _b_   1. boy   _b_   2. cab   _b_   3. double

          p   _p_   4. pet   _p_   5. competent   _p_   6. rip

          d   _d_   7. strand   _d_   8. day   _j_   9. soldier

          n   _n_   10. twinkle   _n_   11. dan   _n_   12. name

          k   _k_   13. kite   _k_   14. wrinkle   _k_   15. wink

          f   _v_   16. of   _f_   17. fun   _f_   18. after

MASTERY REQUIREMENT: 16 correct responses

Indicate mastery on the student response sheet with a check.

ADVANCED LEVEL—Part One

II. WORD ATTACK SKILLS

Name _____

A. Knows Consonant Sounds

1. Initial single
    consonants of
    one sound

Date _____

Mastery 1: _____

4. Medial sounds
5. Final sounds

4: _____

5: _____

DIRECTIONS: The consonants shown in the left column are used in the initial, middle, and
final positions in the words of the same line. Underline the designated consonant in each word, then write its sound in the space provided.

Example: g   _g_   young   _j_   gem   _j_   age

b   ____   1. boy   ____   2. cab   ____   3. double

p   ____   4. pet   ____   5. competent   ____   6. rip

d   ____   7. strand   ____   8. day   ____   9. soldier

n   ____   10. twinkle   ____   11. dan   ____   12. name

k   ____   13. kite   ____   14. wrinkle   ____   15. wink

f   ____   16. of   ____   17. fun   ____   18. after

II. WORD ATTACK SKILLS   A. Knows Consonant Sounds   1. Initial single consonants of one sound

OBJECTIVE: The student will demonstrate that he/she knows the sounds of initial single consonants of one sound.

DIRECTIONS: Read the list of words carefully. Group the words by initial single consonants.

ransom	rampage	runner
frontier	problem	porpoise
purpose	sincere	feud
fiction	hourly	mouth
mammal	jump	puppet
soar	hamburger	former
hassle	juicy	munch
juniper	miracle	simple
raisin	jack	heights

KEY:

raisin, runner, rampage, ransom

purpose, problem, porpoise, puppet

frontier, fiction, former, feud

mammal, miracle, munch, mouth

soar, sincere, simple

hassle, hourly, heights, hamburger

juicy, jump, juniper, jack

MASTERY REQUIREMENT: All correct

Indicate mastery on student response sheet with a check.

ADVANCED LEVEL—Part One

II. WORD ATTACK SKILLS

Name _____

A. Knows Consonant
    Sounds

Date _____

1. Initial single consonants
    of one sound

Mastery _____

DIRECTIONS: Read the list of words carefully. Group the words by initial single consonants.

ransom	rampage	runner
frontier	problem	porpoise
purpose	sincere	feud
fiction	hourly	mouth
mammal	jump	puppet
soar	hamburger	former
hassle	juicy	munch
juniper	miracle	simple
raisin	jack	heights

_____

_____

_____

_____

_____

_____

II. WORD ATTACK SKILLS   A.   Knows Consonant Sounds   2.   Sounds of C and G

OBJECTIVE: The student will demonstrate that he/she knows the sounds of the letters C and G.

DIRECTIONS: Write each word in the space provided using the correct spelling.

club	1. klŭb	decay	11. di kā
cab	2. kăb	gym	12. jĭm
guide	3. gīd	comic	13. kŏm′ ĭk
attic	4. at′ ik	giant	14. jī′ ănt
gay	5. gā	go	15. gō
clay	6. klā	city	16. sĭt′ ē
cyclone	7. sī′ klōn	center	17. sĕn tər
leg	8. lĕg	ginger	18. jĭn jər
gum	9. gŭm	rage	19. rāj
plastic	10. plas′ tik	gauge	20. gāj

MASTERY REQUIREMENT: 16 correct responses

Indicate mastery on the student response sheet with a check.

ADVANCED LEVEL–Part One

II. WORD ATTACK SKILLS

Name _____

    A.   Knows Consonant Sounds

Date _____

      2.   Sounds of C and G

Mastery _____

DIRECTIONS: Write each word in the space provided using the correct spelling.

_____ 1. klŭb

_____ 2. kăb

_____ 3. gīd

_____ 4. at′ ik

_____ 5. gā

_____ 6. klā

_____ 7. sī′ klōn

_____ 8. lĕg

_____ 9. gŭm

_____ 10. plas′ tik

_____ 11. di kā

_____ 12. jĭm

_____ 13. kŏm′ ĭk

_____ 14. jī′ ănt

_____ 15. gō

_____ 16. sĭt′ ē

_____ 17. sĕn tər

_____ 18. jĭn jər

_____ 19. rāj

_____ 20. gāj

II. WORD ATTACK SKILLS   A.   Knows Consonant Sounds   3a.   Blends

OBJECTIVE: The student will demonstrate that he/she knows the sounds of consonant blends.

DIRECTIONS: Many small words and many syllables are made up of a vowel and a cluster of consonant letters on each side. Because these clusters of consonants are pronounced together, or blended, they seem to make one sound and are called consonant blends. Underline the consonant blend in each of the following words.

1. brass
2. secret
3. drum
4. refrain
5. engrave
6. prop
7. scrap
8. emblem
9. class
10. strip
11. inflate
12. glass
13. asleep

14. scum
15. split
16. spring
17. skate
18. small
19. snip
20. inspire
21. trap
22. lobster
23. swine
24. dwell
25. twin

MASTERY REQUIREMENT: 20 correct responses

Indicate mastery on the student response sheet with a check.

ADVANCED LEVEL—Part One

II. WORD ATTACK SKILLS

    A. Knows Consonant Sounds

        3a. Blends

Name _____

Date _____

Mastery _____

DIRECTIONS: Many small words and many syllables are made up of a vowel and a cluster of consonant letters on each side. Because these clusters of consonants are pronounced together, or blended, they seem to make one sound and are called consonant blends. Underline the consonant blend in each of the following words.

1. brass	14. scum
2. secret	15. split
3. drum	16. spring
4. refrain	17. skate
5. engrave	18. small
6. prop	19. snip
7. scrap	20. inspire
8. emblem	21. trap
9. class	22. lobster
10. strip	23. swine
11. inflate	24. dwell
12. glass	25. twin
13. asleep	

II. WORD ATTACK SKILLS   A.   Knows Consonant Sounds   3b. c. **Digraphs, dipthongs**

OBJECTIVE: The student will demonstrate that he/she knows the sounds of digraphs and diphthongs.

DIRECTIONS: Consonant letters which combine to form a new sound are called a digraph. A diphthong is the sound made by gliding continuously between two vowels within the same syllable, like oy in boy.

Read the words below. Underline the digraphs and the diphthongs. On the blank lines write A if the underlined letters form a digraph and B if they form a diphthong.

A	1.	whistle		A	11.	think
A	2.	dash		A	12.	child
B	3.	great		A	13.	chef
A	4.	shop		A	14.	witch
B	5.	play		B	15.	oil
B	6.	glee		B	16.	loyal
A	7.	chew		B	17.	fault
B	8.	boat		B	18.	feel
B	9.	foe		A	19.	dash
A	10.	phone		A	20.	crutch

MASTERY REQUIREMENT: 16 correct responses

Indicate mastery on the student response sheet with a check.

II. WORD ATTACK SKILLS

    A. Knows Consonant Sounds

        3b. c. Digraph,
             dipthong

Name _____

Date _____

Mastery _____

DIRECTIONS: Consonant letters which combine to form a new sound are called a digraph. A diphthong is the sound made by gliding continuously between two vowels within the same syllable, like oy in boy.

Read the words below. Underline the digraphs and the diphthongs. On the blank lines write A if the underlined letters form a digraph and B if they form a diphthong.

____	1.	whistle	____	11.	think
____	2.	dash	____	12.	child
____	3.	great	____	13.	chef
____	4.	shop	____	14.	witch
____	5.	play	____	15.	oil
____	6.	glee	____	16.	loyal
____	7.	chew	____	17.	fault
____	8.	boat	____	18.	feel
____	9.	foe	____	19.	dash
____	10.	phone	____	20.	crutch

II. WORD ATTACK SKILLS   A. Knows Consonant Sounds   4. Medial sounds

OBJECTIVE: The student will demonstrate that he/she knows the medial consonant sounds.

DIRECTIONS: Choose any five of the following consonants: b - d - g - k - n - t - y - h - l - f. Now write four words for each of the five consonants you selected with that consonant sound as the medial sound.

Example: <u>k</u>   market   basket   racket

1. ____   _____   _____   _____   _____

2. ____   _____   _____   _____   _____

3. ____   _____   _____   _____   _____

4. ____   _____   _____   _____   _____

5. ____   _____   _____   _____   _____

MASTERY REQUIREMENT: 16 correct responses

Indicate mastery on the student response sheet with a check.

ADVANCED LEVEL—Part One

II. WORD ATTACK SKILLS

Name _____

A. Knows Consonant Sounds

Date _____

4. Medial sounds

Mastery _____

DIRECTIONS: Choose any five of the following consonants: b - d - g - k - n - t - y - h - l - f. Now write four words for each of the five consonants you selected with that consonant sound as the medial sound.

Example: k   market   basket   racket

1. ____   _____   _____   _____   _____

2. ____   _____   _____   _____   _____

3. ____   _____   _____   _____   _____

4. ____   _____   _____   _____   _____

5. ____   _____   _____   _____   _____

II. WORD ATTACK SKILLS   A. Knows Consonant Sounds   5. Final sounds

OBJECTIVE: The student will demonstrate that he/she knows the sounds of final consonants.

DIRECTIONS: Read the list of words carefully. Underline only the final consonant sound in the word. If the word does not end with a consonant sound, do not make a mark of any kind.

1. fell
2. mate
3. sink
4. concern
5. yap
6. duke
7. asphalt
8. mining
9. politics
10. minute

11. class
12. swim
13. trapper
14. tax
15. hello
16. canoe
17. greetings
18. long
19. shot
20. hourly

MASTERY REQUIREMENT: All Correct

Indicate mastery on the student response sheet with a check.

II. WORD ATTACK SKILLS

Name _____

A. Knows Consonant Sounds

Date _____

5. Final sounds

Mastery _____

DIRECTIONS: Read the list of words carefully. Underline only the final consonant sound in the word. If the word does not end with a consonant sound, do not make a mark of any kind.

1.	fell	11.	class
2.	mate	12.	swim
3.	sink	13.	trapper
4.	concern	14.	tax
5.	yap	15.	hello
6.	duke	16.	canoe
7.	asphalt	17.	greetings
8.	mining	18.	long
9.	politics	19.	shot
10.	minute	20.	hourly

II. WORD ATTACK SKILLS   B. Hears and Can Make Vowel Sounds   1. Long vowels, short vowels

OBJECTIVE: The student will demonstrate that he/she hears and can make long vowels and short vowels.

DIRECTIONS: Read the words in the left column carefully, then place a breve (˘) over the short vowel sounds and a macron (‾) over the long vowel sounds. Next, look at the words in the right column. Write each word phonetically, using the macron (‾) where needed.

Example: kīnd   Example: sweat (swet)
           pĭg   bow   (bō)
           rōpe   nose   (nōz)

1. rāin   11. mow   (mō   )

2. pĕt   12. ewe   (ū   )

3. hē   13. deaf   (def   )

4. sōld   14. plaid (plad   )

5. tēeth   15. fume   (fūm   )

6. thĭck   16. yacht (yot   )

7. nŭt   17. yolk   (yōk   )

8. lĭttle   18. beau   (bō   )

9. cāke   19. braid (brād   )

10. wīld   20. ton   (tun   )

MASTERY REQUIREMENT: 14 correct responses

Indicate mastery on the student response sheet with a check.

II. WORD ATTACK SKILLS

Name _____

B. Hears and Can Make Vowel Sounds

Date _____

1. Long vowels, short vowels

Mastery _____

DIRECTIONS: Read the words in the left column carefully, then place a breve (˘) over the short vowel sounds and a macron (‾) over the long vowel sounds. Next, look at the words in the right column, Write each word phonetically, using the macron (‾) where needed.

Example: kīnd

Example: sweat (swet)

pĭg

bow (bō)

rōpe

nose (nōz)

1. rain

11. mow ( )

2. pet

12. ewe ( )

3. he

13. deaf ( )

4. sold

14. plaid ( )

5. teeth

15. fume ( )

6. thick

16. yacht ( )

7. nut

17. yolk ( )

8. little

18. beau ( )

9. cake

19. braid ( )

10. wild

20. ton ( )

II. WORD ATTACK SKILLS   B. Hears and Can Make Vowel Sounds   2. Can apply
                                                                              vowel rules

OBJECTIVE: The pupil will apply vowel rules.

DIRECTIONS: Read the vowel rule, then mark the sound of the vowels in the words that
                follow. Long vowel (¯), short vowel (˘), silent vowel (/).

A. A single vowel at the beginning or in the middle of a one-syllable word is usually short.

    1. ădd   2. hăm   3. bĕnd   4. ĭt

B. A single vowel at the end of a one-syllable word is usually long.

    5. ā   6. mē   7. gō   8. crȳ

C. When two vowels are together in a one-syllable word, the first vowel is usually long and the
    second is silent.

    9. pāin   10. stēal   11. cūe   12. flōat

D. When there are two vowels in a one-syllable word and one is a final e, the first is usually long
    and the second is silent.

    13. hāte   14. mīne   15. ūse   16. thēse

E. A vowel followed by rr is usually short.

    17. bărrel   18. mĭrror   19. ĕrror   20. bŏrrow

MASTERY REQUIREMENT: 18 correct responses

Indicate mastery on the student response sheet with a check.

II. WORD ATTACK SKILLS

Name _____

B. Hears and Can Make
    Vowel Sounds

Date _____

2. Can apply vowel rules

Mastery _____

DIRECTIONS: Read the vowel rule, then mark the sound of the vowels in the words that follow. Long vowel (⎯), short vowel (∪), silent vowel (/).

A. A single vowel at the beginning or in the middle of a one-syllable word is usually short.

1. add   2. ham   3. bend   4. it

B. A single vowel at the end of a one-syllable word is usually long.

5. a   6. me   7. go   8. cry

C. When two vowels are together in a one-syllable word, the first vowel is usually long and the second is silent.

9. pain   10. steal   11. cue   12. float

D. When there are two vowels in a one-syllable word and one is a final e, the first is usually long and the second is silent.

13. hate   14. mine   15. use   16. these

E. A vowel followed by rr is usually short.

17. barrel   18. mirror   19. error   20. borrow

ADVANCED LEVEL—Part One

II.   WORD ATTACK SKILLS   C.   Knows Elements of Syllabication   1.   Knows rules
                                                                       2.   Can apply
                                                                            rules

OBJECTIVE: The student will demonstrate that he/she knows the rules of syllabication and can apply them.

DIRECTIONS: Study the following set of words. Notice the vowels. Write a rule concerning vowels in syllables.

mo / ment   pu / pil   go   a   he / ro

Rule   (Every syllable contains a vowel.) _____

_____

DIRECTIONS: Study this second set of words. Notice the suffix in each word. Write a rule pertaining to the treatment of suffixes in syllabication.

fast/er   op/tion   last/ly   o/pin/ion   lone/ly

Rule   (When a word contains a suffix, the suffix is the last syllable of the word.) _____

_____

DIRECTIONS: Divide the twelve numbered words that follow into syllables by making a slash mark (/) between the appropriate letters.

1. un / made   7. g o

2. hill / top   8. pro / po / nent

3. gym / nas / tics   9. ar / tis / tic

4. me / ter   10. lone / ly

5. op / tion   11. per / haps

6. o / pin / ion   12. cal / cu / late

MASTERY REQUIREMENT: 1 rule and 11 words correct

Indicate mastery on the student response sheet with a check.

ADVANCED LEVEL—Part One

II. WORD ATTACK SKILLS   Name _____

   C. Knows Elements of
       Syllabication   Date _____

       1. Knows rules
       2. Can apply rules   Mastery (1) _____

                                                   (2) _____

DIRECTIONS: Study the following set of words. Notice the vowels. Write a rule concerning vowels in syllables.

mo/ment   pu/pil   go   a   he/ro

Rule _____

_____

DIRECTIONS: Study this second set of words. Notice the suffix in each word. Write a rule pertaining to the treatment of suffixes in syllabication.

fast/er   op/tion   last/ly   o/pin/ion   lone/ly

Rule _____

_____

DIRECTIONS: Divide the twelve numbered words that follow into syllables by making a slash mark (/) between the appropriate letters.

1. u n m a d e

2. h i l l t o p

3. g y m n a s t i c s

4. m e t e r

5. o p t i o n

6. o p i n i o n

7. g o

8. p r o p o n e n t

9. a r t i s t i c

10. l o n e l y

11. p e r h a p s

12. c a l c u l a t e

II.   WORD ATTACK SKILLS   D.   Uses Accent Properly   1.   Knows and applies rules

OBJECTIVE: The student will demonstrate that he/she knows and can apply accent rules.

DIRECTIONS: Divide the following words into syllables using a slash mark (/); then apply accent rules by inserting an accent mark (′) at the end of each syllable which requires stress.

    1. e n / g a g e ′

    2. s i m ′/ p l y

    3. c a p ′/ t a i n

    4. u n / s t e a d ′/ y

    5. c o ′/ b r a

    6. d e / t a i l e d ′

    7. r e / t u r n ′

    8. b e / s i d e ′

    9. i n / v o l v e d ′

    10. f a ′/ t a l

MASTERY REQUIREMENT: 8 correct responses

Indicate mastery on the student response sheet with a check.

ADVANCED LEVEL—Part One

II. WORD ATTACK SKILLS

Name _____

D. Uses Accent Properly

1. Knows and applies
rules

Date _____

Mastery _____

DIRECTIONS: Divide the following words into syllables using a slash mark (/); then apply accent rules by inserting an accent mark (′) at the end of each syllable which requires stress.

1. e n g a g e

2. s i m p l y

3. c a p t a i n

4. u n s t e a d y

5. c o b r a

6. d e t a i l e d

7. r e t u r n

8. b e s i d e

9. i n v o l v e d

10. f a t a l

II. WORD ATTACK SKILLS   D.   Uses Accent Properly   2.   Can shift accent and
                                                                      change use of word

OBJECTIVE: The student will be able to shift accent to change the use of words.

DIRECTIONS: In each of the following sentences divide the underlined word into syllables,
               then insert an accent mark (´) to show the syllable needing stress, as used in
               that sentence.

1.   After a short rest period, he directed the group to p r o / c e e d́ on their journey.

2.   She collected the p r ó/ c e e d s from the sale.

3.   He entered the c o ń / t e s t with great confidence.

4.   She was determined to c o n / t e s t́ the decision.

5.   The c o ń / f e r / e n c e was informative.

6.   They were asked to c o n / f e ŕ immediately.

7.   She was c o n / t e n t́ with her life.

8.   The c o ń / t e n t of the package is unknown.

9.   His nature was to r e / b e ĺ.

10. The r e b́ / e l soldier fought for a lost cause.

MASTERY REQUIREMENT: 8 correct responses

Indicate mastery on the student response sheet with a check.

ADVANCED LEVEL—Part One

II. WORD ATTACK SKILLS

Name _____

    D. Uses Accent Properly

Date _____

        2. Can shift accent and
            change use of word

Mastery _____

DIRECTIONS: In each of the following sentences divide the underlined word into syllables, then insert an accent mark (´) to show the syllable needing stress, as used in that sentence.

1. After a short rest period, he directed the group to p r o c e e d on their journey.

2. She collected the p r o c e e d s from the sale.

3. He entered the c o n t e s t with great confidence.

4. She was determined to c o n t e s t the decision.

5. The c o n f e r e n c e was informative.

6. They were asked to c o n f e r immediately.

7. She was c o n t e n t with her life.

8. The c o n t e n t of the package is unknown.

9. His nature was to r e b e l.

10. The r e b e l soldier fought for a lost cause.

III. COMPREHENSION   A. **Understands Structure of Story or Paragraph: main idea, topic sentence, sequence of ideas, subordinate ideas**

OBJECTIVE: The student will demonstrate that he/she understands the structure of a story or paragraph by identifying the main idea, the topic sentence, the sequence of ideas, and subordinate ideas.

DIRECTIONS: As you read the following story, look for (1) the main idea, (2) the topic sentence, (3) the sequence of ideas, and (4) subordinate ideas. For item number 1 below, check (√) the statement that best describes the main idea of the passage. For items 2, 3, and 4, write the sentence numbers in the spaces provided to indicate your answer.

[1] Teaching through the medium of television is not as effective as live teaching. [2] The television teacher teaches an unseen audience; therefore, he can not adjust his presentation in response to puzzled looks on the faces of students. [3] He must hope that his listeners understand what he is trying to explain. [4] Neither can students ask questions if the lecturer leaves some points unclarified. [5] The personal touch—knowing that a live person is speaking to you helps to hold the student's attention. [6] It is obvious that a short doze or diverted attention will go undetected by the television teacher. [7] A live teacher will note the lack of attention and call the students' thoughts back to the subject. [8] Finally, the live teacher can engage his students in a discussion of the topic, thereby developing a deeper and more thorough understanding of the subject. [9] Television can be a useful teaching device, but it can never take the place of an effective teacher in the classroom.

Main Idea

1.   The best statement of main idea is:

_____   The personal touch is valuable.

_____   A lecturer needs to see his students.

__√__   Television teaching is less effective than live teaching.

Topic Sentence

2.   __1__   Write the number of the topic sentence.

Sequence of Ideas

3.   __1, 2, 4, 5, 8, 9__   Write the number of each major idea in the passage. List the number in the sequence in which the ideas were presented.

Subordinate Ideas

4.   ___3, 6, 7___   Write the number of each subordinate idea presented in the passage.

MASTERY REQUIREMENT: Main Idea—correct, Topic sentence—correct, Sequence of Ideas 5 correct, Subordinate Ideas—3 correct

Indicate mastery on the student response sheet with a check.

III. COMPREHENSION

A. Understands Structure
of Story or Paragraph:
main idea, topic sentence,
sequence of ideas,
subordinate ideas

Name _____

Date _____

Mastery:
Main Idea _____
Topic Sentence _____
Sequence of Ideas _____
Subordinate Ideas _____

DIRECTIONS: As you read the following story, look for (1) the main idea, (2) the topic sentence, (3) the sequence of ideas, and (4) subordinate ideas. For item number 1 below, check (√) the statement that best describes the main idea of the passage. For items 2, 3, and 4, write the sentence numbers in the spaces provided to indicate your answer.

[1] Teaching through the medium of television is not as effective as live teaching. [2] The television teacher teaches an unseen audience; therefore, he can not adjust his presentation in response to puzzled looks on the faces of students. [3] He must hope that his listeners understand what he is trying to explain. [4] Neither can students ask questions if the lecturer leaves some points unclarified. [5] The personal touch—knowing that a live person is speaking to you helps to hold the student's attention. [6] It is obvious that a short doze or diverted attention will go undetected by the television teacher. [7] A live teacher will note the lack of attention and call the students' thoughts back to the subject. [8] Finally, the live teacher can engage his students in a discussion of the topic, thereby developing a deeper and more thorough understanding of the subject. [9] Television can be a useful teaching device, but it can never take the place of an effective teacher in the classroom.

Main Idea

1. The best statement of main idea is:

_____ The personal touch is valuable.

_____ A lecturer needs to see his students.

_____ Television teaching is less effective than live teaching.

Topic Sentence

2. _____ Write the number of the topic sentence.

Sequence of Ideas

3. _____ Write the number of each major idea in the passage. List the number in the sequence in which the ideas were presented.

Subordinate Ideas

4. _____ Write the number of each subordinate idea presented in the passage.

III. COMPREHENSION   B.   Can Repeat General Idea of Material Read
                         C.   Can Remember Specific Important Facts
                         D.   Can Relate Material Read to Known Information
                              or Experience

OBJECTIVE: After reading a short passage, the student will repeat the general idea of the
                material read, remember specific facts and relate the material read to known
                information or experience.

DIRECTIONS: Read the story below carefully. Then answer the questions that follow.

   Jim and his friend Charlie had just awakened from a night of camping on the south side of
town. Jim stretched and yawned. Today was one of those mornings one experiences after having
too little sleep.
   Jim was hungry, but he just remembered that in his eagerness to get to the campsite he had
forgotten to bring food.
   "Charlie," he said drowsily, "do you have anything to eat?"
   "Naw," said Charlie, "nothing but some lollipops."
   "Gimme one," said Jim.
   Charlie handed a yellow lollipop to Jim who unwrapped it at a speed that equaled his
eagerness to attack the new day.
   "Wow, this thing is sour!" Jim exclaimed as he jumped up.
   "I could sure use some hot cakes, syrup and sausage," Jim said. "Let's head for home and
see what we can round up. That's the last lollipop I will ever want for breakfast."

B.   Briefly state the general idea of the passage.

     (The behavior or reaction of a boy following a night of camping. OR Boys camping and how

     they felt in the morning OR similar statement)
     _____

C.   List six (6) specific, important facts.
     1.   (Jim and Charlie were camping)
     2.   (Jim was tired.)
     3.   (Jim was hungry.)
     4.   (He had forgotten to bring food.)
     5.   (Charlie had lollipops.)
     6.   (The lollipop was sour.)
     7.   (Jim wanted to go home and eat breakfast.)
     8.   (Jim did not want any more lollipops for breakfast.)

D.   Using past experiences and information, answer the following questions:
     1.   Did Jim and Charlie get a good night's sleep? _____ (No)
     2.   How did Jim feel when he awoke? _____ (tired)
     3.   What effect did the sour lollipop have on Jim? _____ (made him alert)
     4.   Why does Jim not want any more lollipops for breakfast? _____ (They are sour.)
          _____ (They are not good for breakfast)

MASTERY REQUIREMENT: B—general idea correct, C—6 important facts, D—3 acceptable
                       responses

Indicate mastery on the student response sheet with a check.

ADVANCED LEVEL—Part One

III. COMPREHENSION

Name _____

B. Can Repeat General Idea
of Material Read

Date _____

C. Can Remember Specific
Important Facts

D. Can Relate Material Read
to Known Information or
Experience

Mastery   B. _____
          C. _____
          D. _____

DIRECTIONS: Read the story below carefully. Then answer the questions that follow.

Jim and his friend Charlie had just awakened from a night of camping on the south side of town. Jim stretched and yawned. Today was one of those mornings one experiences after having too little sleep.

Jim was hungry, but he just remembered that in his eagerness to get to the campsite he had forgotten to bring food.

"Charlie," he said drowsily, "do you have anything to eat?"

"Naw," said Charlie, "nothing but some lollipops."

"Gimme one," said Jim.

Charlie handed a yellow lollipop to Jim who unwrapped it at a speed that equaled his eagerness to attack the new day.

"Wow, this thing is sour!" Jim exclaimed as he jumped up.

"I could sure use some hot cakes, syrup and sausage," Jim said. "Let's head for home and see what we can round up. That's the last lollipop I will ever want for breakfast."

B. Briefly state the general idea of the passage.

_____

_____

_____

C. List six (6) specific, important facts.

_____

_____

_____

_____

_____

_____

D. Using past experiences and information, answer the following questions:

1. Did Jim and Charlie get a good night's sleep? _____

2. How did Jim feel when he awoke? _____

3. What effect did the sour lollipop have on Jim? _____

4. Why does Jim not want any more lollipops for breakfast? _____

_____

III. COMPREHENSION E. Can Follow Printed Directions

OBJECTIVE: The student will demonstrate he/she can follow printed directions.

DIRECTIONS: Read the following directions and record your responses below each one.

1. Draw three circles.

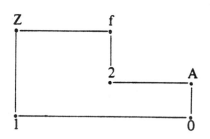

2. Print the first 10 letters of the alphabet.

3. Write your full name in this order: last name, first name, middle.

4. Place the point of your pencil on the dot marked "1." Draw a line to dot "Z." Draw a line to "f," then "2," then "A," then "0" and back to "1."

MASTERY REQUIREMENT: 4 correct responses

Indicate mastery on the student response sheet with a check.

ADVANCED LEVEL—Part One

III. COMPREHENSION

    E.   Can Follow Printed
         Directions

Name _____

Date _____

Mastery _____

DIRECTIONS: Read the following directions and record your responses below each one.

1.   Draw three circles.

2.   Print the first 10 letters of the alphabet.

3.   Write your full name in this order: last name, first name, middle.

4.   Place the point of your pencil on the dot marked "1." Draw a line to dot "Z." Draw a
line to "f," then "2," then "A," then "0" and back to "1."

          Z.   f.

               2.   A.

           1.   0.

III. COMPREHENSION   F. Can Interpret Hidden Meaning

OBJECTIVE: The student will demonstrate the ability to interpret hidden meaning.

DIRECTIONS: Read the following passages. Decide what the hidden meaning is in each one, and explain the hidden meaning in the space below.

1. If I am elected Student Council President, I promise to give you, for the first time in the history of this school, a loud voice in student government.

    (Students have not previously had a part in determining how they would be governed.)

2. You never miss your water until the well runs dry.

    (A person fails to appreciate what he has until he loses it.)

3. Don't count your chickens before they hatch.

    (A person should not depend on getting something until he actually has it.)

MASTERY REQUIREMENT: #1 correct and *either* #2 or #3 correct

Indicate mastery on the student response sheet with a check.

III.   COMPREHENSION

   F.   Can Interpret Hidden
        Meaning

Name _____

Date _____

Mastery _____

DIRECTIONS: Read the following passages. Decide what the hidden meaning is in each one, and explain the hidden meaning in the space below.

1.   If I am elected Student Council President, I promise to give you, for the first time in the history of this school, a loud voice in student government.

2.   You never miss your water until the well runs dry.

3.   Don't count your chickens before they hatch.

IV.   SILENT AND ORAL READING   A.   Reads Silently without Lip Movements
                                   B.   Reads Silently at Twice Oral Rate
                                   C.   Adjusts Silent Rate to Material
                                        1.   Reads popular fiction at 200+ words per
                                             minute

OBJECTIVE: The pupil will read silently without lip movement, read at twice the oral rate, and read fiction at 200+ words per minute.

DIRECTIONS: Time the student while he or she reads the following story. Have him/her read for one (1) minute. Observe the student as he/she reads to determine if there are lip movements. At the end of one minute—

SAY: STOP—Mark the last word that you read.

THE CLAM BAKE

12	Have you ever gone to a clam bake? That is great fun.
28	When I was visiting in Hartford, my friend suggested that we go out to a clam
44	bake. A large number of kids from the neighborhood had been invited and a bus had
60	been chartered to take us to an outlying coastal area where the bake would take place.
76	Chris and I boarded the bus shortly after six. We were already hungry from a long
93	day of swimming and playing on the beach, so we could hardly wait to finish off the
99	day with a fine seafood dinner.
115	In our eagerness for food, it seemed that we would never arrive at the clam bake
133	scene. Finally the bus came to a halt. We hurried out of the bus and headed straight for
149	the pavilion where the food would be served. But, to our surprise the food was not
165	there, and a quick survey of the surroundings told us that the clams had not even
166	arrived.
183	As we were about to walk down to the ocean, a small truck pulled into the drive
186	beside the pavilion.
196	"Come on," Chris said, "let's see what's on the truck."
209	The driver had already started unloading. As we approached the truck, I suddenly
220	knew that tonight I would be eating more than just clams.
236	An older gentleman was working over a vat, or long tub-like pan. He poured some
251	water in and put something in that looked like seaweed. Then he put in potatoes,
266	onions and more weed-looking plants, green corn with husks on, and clams and lob-
280	sters. Then he covered all of this strange mixture with a canvas. A fire was quickly
285	built underneath the vat.
297	"How long will it take to cook this food?" I asked Chris.
309	"I don't know," she said, "but it will be worth the wait."

(Continued on page 80)

IV.   SILENT AND ORAL READING

A.   **Reads Silently without Lip Movements**
B.   **Reads Silently at Twice Oral Rate**
C.   **Adjusts Silent Rate to Material**

1.   **Reads popular fiction at 200+ words per minute**

Name _____

Date _____

Mastery   A: _____
          B: _____
          C: _____

DIRECTIONS: Read the following story to yourself.

THE CLAM BAKE

12	Have you ever gone to a clam bake? That is great fun.
28	When I was visiting in Hartford, my friend suggested that we go out to a clam
44	bake. A large number of kids from the neighborhood had been invited and a bus had
60	been chartered to take us to an outlying coastal area where the bake would take place.
76	Chris and I boarded the bus shortly after six. We were already hungry from a long
93	day of swimming and playing on the beach, so we could hardly wait to finish off the
99	day with a fine seafood dinner.
115	In our eagerness for food, it seemed that we would never arrive at the clam bake
133	scene. Finally the bus came to a halt. We hurried out of the bus and headed straight for
149	the pavilion where the food would be served. But, to our surprise the food was not
165	there, and a quick survey of the surroundings told us that the clams had not even
166	arrived.
183	As we were about to walk down to the ocean, a small truck pulled into the drive
186	beside the pavilion.
196	"Come on," Chris said, "let's see what's on the truck."
209	The driver had already started unloading. As we approached the truck, I suddenly
220	knew that tonight I would be eating more than just clams.
236	An older gentleman was working over a vat, or long tub-like pan. He poured some
251	water in and put something in that looked like seaweed. Then he put in potatoes,
266	onions and more weed-looking plants, green corn with husks on, and clams and lob-
280	sters. Then he covered all of this strange mixture with a canvas. A fire was quickly
285	built underneath the vat.
297	"How long will it take to cook this food?" I asked Chris.
309	"I don't know," she said, "but it will be worth the wait."
324	To get our minds off our stomachs we joined a group playing volleyball in the
332	large clearing between the pavilion and the ocean.

(Continued)

324	To get our minds off our stomachs we joined a group playing volleyball in the
332	large clearing between the pavilion and the ocean.
348	I was pretty good at the sport, having played two years on our school team. It
365	was great, as an outsider, to have some skill that could be used to make an impression.
368	And it did.
382	As soon as we stopped playing, a good-looking guy named Eddie said, "Hey,
399	you're pretty good at that game. Come on and show me how good you are at eating
400	clams."
416	"I'll need some instructions in clam eating, I'm sure, so if that is your thing, may-
422	be I should join you," I said.
436	As we approached the area where the food was being served, I suddenly noticed
440	the hunger pains again.
457	The meal was fantastic. First, we picked up a Texas-size plate and got in line. A
474	large potato, two ears of corn, a big lobster, and a pint cardboard cup of clams were
492	placed on the plate. We joined some of the early birds at a table under the pavilion, and
504	it was there that I received my first lesson on eating clams.
521	I must admit that I was not impressed greatly with the taste of clams, but I shall
536	never forget the great taste of sweet lobster meat with drawn butter dripping from it,
553	the corn-on-the-cob, the coolness of the sea breeze, the lingering smell of seafood, and
569	the excited voices of friends as they savored the harvest of the fields and the sea.
577	It was a night I shall never forget.

_____ A. Was there evidence of lip movements?

(Yes–No)

_____ B. How many words were read in one minute?

(Number)

_____ C. Did student read 200 or more words per minute?

(Yes–No)

MASTERY REQUIREMENT: A—No evidence of lip movement
B—400 words per minute
C—200 + words per minute

Indicate mastery on the student response sheet with a check.

348
365
368
I was pretty good at the sport, having played two years on our school team. It was great, as an outsider, to have some skill that could be used to make an impression. And it did.

382
399
400
As soon as we stopped playing, a good-looking guy named Eddie said, "Hey, you're pretty good at that game. Come on and show me how good you are at eating clams."

416
422
"I'll need some instructions in clam eating, I'm sure, so if that is your thing, maybe I should join you," I said.

436
440
As we approached the area where the food was being served, I suddenly noticed the hunger pains again.

457
474
492
504
The meal was fantastic. First, we picked up a Texas-size plate and got in line. A large potato, two ears of corn, a big lobster, and a pint cardboard cup of clams were placed on the plate. We joined some of the early birds at a table under the pavilion, and it was there that I received my first lesson on eating clams.

521
536
553
569
I must admit that I was not impressed greatly with the taste of clams, but I shall never forget the great taste of sweet lobster meat with drawn butter dripping from it, the corn-on-the-cob, the coolness of the sea breeze, the lingering smell of seafood, and the excited voices of friends as they savored the harvest of the fields and the sea.

577
It was a night I shall never forget.

_____ A. Was there evidence of lip movements?
(Yes—No)

_____ B. How many words were read in one minute?
(Number)

_____ C. Did student read 200 or more words per minute?
(Yes—No)

IV.   SILENT AND ORAL READING   C.   Adjusts Silent Rate to Material

2.   Uses skimming techniques when applicable

OBJECTIVE: The student will demonstrate that she/he uses skimming techniques when applicable.

DIRECTIONS: Observe the student over a period of several days or weeks to determine if she/he uses skimming techniques when it is appropriate.

The student uses skimming techniques:

_____   1.   when attempting to locate specific information in books or periodicals.

_____   2.   when finding answers in the text during class discussions.

_____   3.   when searching for words in a dictionary.

_____   4.   when searching for information in an encyclopedia.

_____   5.   when looking for specific locations or information on maps.

_____   6.   when using a glossary.

MASTERY REQUIREMENT: Teacher judgment

Indicate mastery on the student response sheet with a check.

IV.   SILENT AND ORAL READING   Name _____

    C.   **Adjusts Silent Rate to
        Material**   Date _____

        2.   **Uses skimming techniques
            when applicable**   Mastery _____

DIRECTIONS: Observe the student over a period of several days or weeks to determine if she/he uses skimming techniques when it is appropriate.

The student uses skimming techniques:

_____   1.   when attempting to locate specific information in books or periodicals.

_____   2.   when finding answers in the text during class discussions.

_____   3.   when searching for words in a dictionary.

_____   4.   when searching for information in an encyclopedia.

_____   5.   when looking for specific locations or information on maps.

_____   6.   when using a glossary.

IV.   SILENT AND ORAL READING   D.   Eye-Voice Span 3 to 5 Words (in oral reading)
                                  E.   Reads Aloud with Comprehension

OBJECTIVE: The student will demonstrate an eye-voice span of three to five words when
               reading orally, and the ability to read aloud with comprehension.

DIRECTIONS: Read the following story aloud. From time to time, while reading, look up at
               the teacher without breaking your voice pattern. After you have read the story,
               answer the question by checking statements which describe Jim Smith.

A FELLOW NAMED JIM

15   Jim Smith was the kind of person everyone liked. He was a big fellow, about
29   6'3", 225 pounds, and he carried his weight well. He looked like a professional
45   football player or a boxer, but he was neither. As a matter of fact he enjoyed
54   helping someone up much more than knocking him down.

69   Jim had a friendly greeting and a ready smile for everyone he met. I don't
82   suppose that he ever met a stranger. At least it appeared that way.

94   Jim Smith was a picture of health, both physically and mentally. Almost
110   everyone who knew him felt that he was a person without a worry. I recall Bill
125   Roberts, one of the influentials of our town stating that "Jim must be the happiest,
138   most outgoing and contented person around. He is going places," Bill said. "You
156   just watch him. By the time he is thirty-five he will have made his mark on this
157   community."

170   Biff Owens' comments and looks of admiration for Jim will not be forgotten
182   soon by our townspeople. Perhaps Biff was Jim's greatest admirer. Although there
196   were several years' difference in their ages, Jim kind of took Biff, a neighborhood
212   boy, under his wing. Biff's father had died while he was quite young and Jim became
229   a second father to him. He took Biff fishing, played catch with him in the back yard,
245   fixed his bicycle when it would break, and he taught Biff the kind of things that
253   only the best of adults teach their offsprings.

268   Yes, as Bill predicted, Jim Smith made his mark on our small town. He was
283   around only twenty-three years. But each year counted. A lot of people here know
296   a lot more about living than they did before Jim Smith came along.

Jim Smith was:

_____ 1.   an old man   √   6.   big

  √   2.   a young man   _____ 7.   awkward

_____ 3.   a poor man   √   8.   helpful

  √   4.   friendly   _____ 9.   an orphan

  √   5.   outgoing   √   10.   a good teacher

MASTERY REQUIREMENT: 8 correct responses

Indicate mastery on the student response sheet with a check.

IV.   SILENT AND ORAL READING   Name _____

      D.   Eye-Voice Span 3 to 5
           Words (in oral reading)   Date _____
      E.   Reads Aloud with
           Comprehension
                                        Mastery _____

DIRECTIONS: Read the following story aloud. From time to time, while reading, look up at
              the teacher without breaking your voice pattern. After you have read the story,
              answer the question by checking statements which describe Jim Smith.

A FELLOW NAMED JIM

15   Jim Smith was the kind of person everyone liked. He was a big fellow, about
29   6'3", 225 pounds, and he carried his weight well. He looked like a professional
45   football player or a boxer, but he was neither. As a matter of fact he enjoyed
54   helping someone up much more than knocking him down.

69   Jim had a friendly greeting and a ready smile for everyone he met. I don't
82   suppose that he ever met a stranger. At least it appeared that way.

94   Jim Smith was a picture of health, both physically and mentally. Almost
110 everyone who knew him felt that he was a person without a worry. I recall Bill
125 Roberts, one of the influentials of our town stating that "Jim must be the happiest,
138 most outgoing and contented person around. He is going places," Bill said. "You
156 just watch him. By the time he is thirty-five he will have made his mark on this
157 community."

170   Biff Owens' comments and looks of admiration for Jim will not be forgotten
182 soon by our townspeople. Perhaps Biff was Jim's greatest admirer. Although there
196 were several years' difference in their ages, Jim kind of took Biff, a neighborhood
212 boy, under his wing. Biff's father had died while he was quite young and Jim became
229 a second father to him. He took Biff fishing, played catch with him in the back yard,
245 fixed his bicycle when it would break, and he taught Biff the kind of things that
253 only the best of adults teach their offsprings.

268   Yes, as Bill predicted, Jim Smith made his mark on our small town. He was
283 around only twenty-three years. But each year counted. A lot of people here know
296 a lot more about living than they did before Jim Smith came along.

Jim Smith was:

_____ 1. an old man   _____ 6. big

_____ 2. a young man   _____ 7. awkward

_____ 3. a poor man   _____ 8. helpful

_____ 4. friendly   _____ 9. an orphan

_____ 5. outgoing   _____ 10. a good teacher

I. VOCABULARY   A. Increases Vocabulary through Wide Reading

OBJECTIVE: The student will increase his/her vocabulary through wide reading.

DIRECTIONS: The teacher will complete the following checklist for each student by placing a check (√) beside each sentence that describes the student.

The student:

_____ 1. uses the library frequently.

_____ 2. shows interest in acquiring information by selecting books containing varied content.

_____ 3. often has a book to use for free-reading purposes.

_____ 4. often comments about a book he/she is currently reading.

_____ 5. encourages others to read books that he/she has read.

_____ 6. does not complain when given an assignment that requires reading.

_____ 7. is able to relate what is read to everyday life.

MASTERY REQUIREMENT: Teacher judgment

Indicate mastery on the student response sheet with a check.

ADVANCED LEVEL—Part Two

I. VOCABULARY

    A.   Increases Vocabulary
        through Wide Reading

Name _____

Date _____

Mastery _____

DIRECTIONS: The teacher will complete the following checklist for each student by placing a check (√) beside each sentence that describes the student.

The student:

_____   1.   uses the library frequently.

_____   2.   shows interest in acquiring information by selecting books containing varied content.

_____   3.   often has a book to use for free-reading purposes.

_____   4.   often comments about a book he/she is currently reading.

_____   5.   encourages others to read books that he/she has read.

_____   6.   does not complain when given an assignment that requires reading.

_____   7.   is able to relate what is read to everyday life.

ADVANCED LEVEL—Part Two

I. VOCABULARY   B. Organizes Own Word-Study Techniques

OBJECTIVE: The student exhibits organized word-study techniques.

DIRECTIONS: Respond in writing to the following question.

In reading, you sometimes find words that you do not know. What do you do to discover their meanings and pronunciations?

1. _____

2. _____

3. _____

4. _____

5. _____

MASTERY REQUIREMENT: Teacher judgment

Indicate mastery on the student response sheet with a check.

ADVANCED LEVEL—Part Two

I. VOCABULARY   Name _____

    B.   Organizes Own Word-
         Study Techniques   Date _____

                                                  Mastery _____

DIRECTIONS: Respond in writing to the following question.

In reading, you sometimes find words that you do not know. What do you do to discover their meanings and pronunciations?

1. _____

2. _____

3. _____

4. _____

5. _____

ADVANCED LEVEL—Part Two

II.   COMPREHENSION   A.   Interpretation   1.   Sequences events from multiple sources
                                                 2.   Makes generalizations from multiple sources
                                                 3.   Identifies relationships of elements from multiple sources

OBJECTIVE: The student will demonstrate the ability to sequence events, make generalizations, and identify relationships of elements from multiple sources.

DIRECTIONS: Complete the following using the information provided.

      a.   Moon Landing

      b.   America Discovered

      c.   First Crossing of the Rocky Mountains

      d.   Pilgrims at Plymouth

1.   Put these four events in the order in which they happened, using the letters beside each one.

    <u>(b)</u>   <u>(d)</u>   <u>(c)</u>   <u>(a)</u>

2.   Make a general statement in less than ten (10) words about these events.

(They are all historical events.)
(They all have to do with discovery.)

3.   How are all of these events related?

(They all involved America.)
(They all have to do with discovery and exploration.)

MASTERY REQUIREMENT: 3 correct responses

Indicate mastery on the student response sheet with a check.

ADVANCED LEVEL—Part Two

II. COMPREHENSION

Name _____

A. Interpretation

1. Sequences events from multiple sources
2. Makes generalizations from multiple sources
3. Identifies relationships of elements from multiple sources

Date _____

Mastery _____

DIRECTIONS: Complete the following using the information provided.

a. Moon Landing

b. America Discovered

c. First Crossing of the Rocky Mountains

d. Pilgrims at Plymouth

1. Put these four events in the order in which they happened, using the letters beside each one.

_____   _____   _____   _____

2. Make a general statement in less than ten (10) words about these events.

_____

_____

3. How are all of these events related?

_____

_____

_____

II. COMPREHENSION   A. Interpretation   4. Identifies author's purpose

OBJECTIVE: The student will demonstrate his/her ability to identify the author's purpose.

DIRECTIONS: Explain the author's purpose in writing the following passage.

"When casting your vote for Science Club President, you could elect Jim Hall, the fellow who has caused more calamities in the chemistry lab than anyone else. You might vote for Alice Moore, whose only qualification is her long blond hair. Your other choice is the top science student in school."

Explain the author's purpose:

(The author's purpose is to obtain votes.)

MASTERY REQUIREMENT: Teacher judgment

Indicate mastery on the student response sheet with a check.

ADVANCED LEVEL—Part Two

II. COMPREHENSION

    A. Interpretation

        4. Identifies author's
            purpose

Name _____

Date _____

Mastery _____

DIRECTIONS: Explain the author's purpose in writing the following passage.

"When casting your vote for Science Club President, you could elect Jim Hall, the fellow who has caused more calamities in the chemistry lab than anyone else. You might vote for Alice Moore, whose only qualification is her long blond hair. Your other choice is the top science student in school."

Explain the author's purpose:

_____

_____

_____

_____

_____

II. COMPREHENSION   A. Interpretation   5. Develops use of parts of speech
                                                  through transformation of sequences

OBJECTIVE: The student will develop the use of parts of speech through transformation of
sequences.

DIRECTIONS: In each of the following groups of sentences, circle the sentence that communicates the ideas in the harshest way.

1. (a.) Don't slam the door!

    b. I wish you wouldn't slam the door.

    c. Close the door gently, Karen.

2. a. I like Mary Jones least of all.

    b. Mary Jones is not one of my favorite people.

    (c.) I can't stand Mary Jones!

3. a. There's no reason for my teacher to treat me that way.

    b. I wish I knew why my teacher doesn't like me.

    (c.) My teacher hates me!

MASTERY REQUIREMENT: 2 correct responses

Indicate mastery on the student response sheet with a check.

ADVANCED LEVEL—Part Two

II.   COMPREHENSION

   A.   Interpretation

      5.   Develops use of parts
           of speech through
           transformation of
           sequences

Name _____

Date _____

Mastery _____ .

DIRECTIONS: In each of the following groups of sentences, circle the sentence that communi-
              cates the ideas in the harshest way.

   1.   a.   Don't slam the door!

        b.   I wish you wouldn't slam the door.

        c.   Close the door gently, Karen.

   2.   a.   I like Mary Jones least of all.

        b.   Mary Jones is not one of my favorite people.

        c.   I can't stand Mary Jones!

   3.   a.   There's no reason for my teacher to treat me that way.

        b.   I wish I knew why my teacher doesn't like me.

        c.   My teacher hates me!

II. COMPREHENSION   B. Application   1. Uses multiple sources for documentation and support for opinion
2. Uses maps, graphs, charts, tables when appropriate in response to readings
3. Takes notes during debate and other presentations in order to summarize and respond to logic used

OBJECTIVE: The student will show evidence of using multiple sources for documentation, maps, graphs, charts, tables, and note-taking.

DIRECTIONS: Complete the following for each student by checking the statements that describe the student. The teacher should observe the student's performance during regular class assignments or make a specific research assignment which requires these skills and behaviors.

The student:

_____ 1. Uses several sources for documentation of his/her research and support for opinion.

_____ 2. Uses maps, graphs, charts, or tables when they are appropriate in response to readings.

_____ 3. Takes notes in class during lectures, discussions, and other presentations in order to summarize information and respond to the logic used.

MASTERY REQUIREMENT: Teacher judgment

Indicate mastery on the student response sheet with a check.

II. COMPREHENSION

Name _____

B. Application

Date _____

1. Uses multiple sources for documentation and support for opinion

Mastery _____

2. Uses maps, graphs, charts, tables when appropriate in response to readings

3. Takes notes during debate and other presentations in order to summarize and respond to logic used

DIRECTIONS: Complete the following for each student by checking the statements that describe the student. The teacher should observe the student's performance during regular class assignments or make a specific research assignment which requires these skills and behaviors.

The student:

_____ 1. Uses several sources for documentation of his/her research and support for opinion.

_____ 2. Uses maps, graphs, charts, or tables when they are appropriate in response to readings.

_____ 3. Takes notes in class during lectures, discussions, and other presentations in order to summarize information and respond to the logic used.

ADVANCED LEVEL—Part Two

II. COMPREHENSION   B. Application   4. Uses reading for different purposes:
a. practical information
b. problem solving
c. recreation

OBJECTIVE: The student will demonstrate use of reading to obtain practical information, to solve problems, and for recreation.

DIRECTIONS: Which of the following materials would you read for these purposes:
a. to gain practical information
b. for solving a problem
c. for recreation
Place the appropriate letter in the space provided before each type of material.

  c   1. comic books

  a   2. textbooks

  b   3. yellow pages of telephone directory

  b   4. "How to fix it" books

  c   5. fiction

  c   6. popular magazines

  a   7. cookbook

  b   8. dictionary

  a   9. road map

  c   10. biography

  a   11. calendar

  b   12. directions for assembling a machine

MASTERY REQUIREMENT: 9 correct responses

Indicate mastery on the student response sheet with a check.

II. COMPREHENSION

Name _____

B. Application

Date _____

    4. Uses reading for different purposes

Mastery _____

        a. practical information
        b. problem solving
        c. recreation

DIRECTIONS: Which of the following materials would you read for these purposes:
a. to gain practical information
b. for solving a problem
c. for recreation
Place the appropriate letter in the space provided before each type of material.

_____ 1. comic books

_____ 2. textbooks

_____ 3. yellow pages of telephone directory

_____ 4. "How to fix it" books

_____ 5. fiction

_____ 6. popular magazines

_____ 7. cookbook

_____ 8. dictionary

_____ 9. road map

_____ 10. biography

_____ 11. calendar

_____ 12. directions for assembling a machine

II. COMPREHENSION   C. Analysis   1. Differentiates between types of sentences:

        a. expository
        b. narrative
        c. descriptive
        d. persuasive

OBJECTIVE: The student will differentiate between expository, narrative, descriptive and persuasive sentences.

DIRECTIONS: Each of the sentences below is either expository (explanatory), narrative, descriptive, or persuasive in nature. The student will decide which kind each sentence is and indicate the kind by writing the appropriate letter before each sentence.

        a. expository
        b. narrative
        c. descriptive
        d. persuasive

__c__ 1. The beautiful blue jays were chattering noisily.

__b__ 2. One day three men set out on a journey across the Andes Mountains.

__d__ 3. "Let me sell you the house on the hill, and you will have a lovely view of the valley."

__c__ 4. The new building will be made of steel and have a brick entrance with sidewalks leading to each doorway.

__a__ 5. The best way to win friends is to be friendly.

__d__ 6. "If you will drive me home, I will repay you many times."

__c__ 7. The corners of his mouth began to curl upward, then he suddenly burst into a belly-type laughter.

__a__ 8. To reach point A, one must proceed east two hundred feet, turn left and follow the arrows.

__d__ 9. "A vote for John Doe will assure you of honesty in government."

__b__ 10. Jane drove down the street looking for 1100 Madison Avenue.

MASTERY REQUIREMENT: 8 correct responses

Indicate mastery on the student reponse sheet with a check.

II.   COMPREHENSION

C.   Analysis

1. Differentiates between types of sentences:

a. expository
b. narrative
c. descriptive
d. persuasive

Name _____

Date _____

Mastery _____

DIRECTIONS: Each of the sentences below is either expository (explanatory), narrative, descriptive, or persuasive in nature. Decide which kind each sentence is and indicate the kind by writing the appropriate letter before each sentence.

a. expository
b. narrative
c. descriptive
d. persuasive

_____ 1.   The beautiful blue jays were chattering noisily.

_____ 2.   One day three men set out on a journey across the Andes Mountains.

_____ 3.   "Let me sell you the house on the hill, and you will have a lovely view of the valley."

_____ 4.   The new building will be made of steel and have a brick entrance with sidewalks leading to each doorway.

_____ 5.   The best way to win friends is to be friendly.

_____ 6.   "If you will drive me home, I will repay you many times."

_____ 7.   The corners of his mouth began to curl upward, then he suddenly burst into a belly-type laughter.

_____ 8.   To reach point A, one must proceed east two hundred feet, turn left and follow the arrows.

_____ 9.   "A vote for John Doe will assure you of honesty in government."

_____10.   Jane drove down the street looking for 1100 Madison Avenue.

II. COMPREHENSION   D. Synthesis   1. Extends generalizations beyond sources
                                          2. Hypothesizes
                                          3. Suggests alternatives and options

OBJECTIVE: The student will show evidence of synthesizing materials read by generalizing beyond the sources, by hypothesizing, and by suggesting alternatives and options.

DIRECTIONS: Read the information below, then respond to the questions that follow.

The average yield of corn in the United States is fifty-four (54) bushels per acre. In Central Oklahoma the yield occasionally averages seventy (70) bushels per acre; however, most years it is quite low, about twenty (20) bushels.

In recent years, much thought has been given to irrigating this region. One possibility for acquiring water is to drill deep wells. Perhaps there are other solutions to the farm problem here.

1. Extends generalizations (check your response)
    a. The major farm problem is:
        __✓__ (1) lack of rain
        _____ (2) excessive heat
        _____ (3) poor farm land
               (4) problem unknown
    b. Corn yield could be increased by:
        _____ (1) proper fertilization
        _____ (2) early planting
        __✓__ (3) irrigation
        _____ (4) don't know

2. Hypothesizes
    a. Through irrigation one might expect:
        _____ (1) a yield of 54 bushels per acre
        __✓__ (2) a yield of 70 bushels per acre
        _____ (3) no increase in yield

3. Alternatives
    a. Possible alternatives to drilling wells are:
        __✓__ (1) building lakes to catch rain water
        __✓__ (2) planting crops that require less water
        _____ (3) other—list

MASTERY REQUIREMENT: 1—two correct responses
                      2—correct
                      3—two alternatives

Indicate mastery on the student response sheet with a check.

II.   COMPREHENSION

    D.   Synthesis

       1.   Extends generalizations
          beyond sources
       2.   Hypothesizes
       3.   Suggests alternatives
          and options

Name _____

Date _____.

Mastery   1. _____
           2. _____
           3. _____

DIRECTIONS: Read the information below, then respond to the questions that follow.

The average yield of corn in the United States is fifty-four (54) bushels per acre. In Central Oklahoma the yield occasionally averages seventy (70) bushels per acre; however, most years it is quite low, about twenty (20) bushels.

In recent years, much thought has been given to irrigating this region. One possibility for acquiring water is to drill deep wells. Perhaps there are other solutions to the farm problem here.

1.   Extends generalizations (check your response)

    a.   The major farm problem is:

        _____ (1)   lack of rain

        _____ (2)   excessive heat

        _____ (3)   poor farm land

        _____ (4)   problem unknown

    b.   Corn yield could be increased by:

        _____ (1)   proper fertilization

        _____ (2)   early planting

        _____ (3)   irrigation

        _____ (4)   don't know

2.   Hypothesizes

    a.   Through irrigation one might expect:

        _____ (1)   a yield of 54 bushels per acre

        _____ (2)   a yield of 70 bushels per acre

        _____ (3)   no increase in yield

3.   Alternatives

    a.   Possible alternatives to drilling wells are:

        _____ (1)   building lakes to catch rain water

        _____ (2)   planting crops that require less water

        _____ (3)   other—list

II. COMPREHENSION   E. Critical Evaluation   1. Develops own criteria for critical review of materials:
 a. fiction
 b. propaganda
 c. nonfiction
 d. essays
 e. journals
 f. biographies

OBJECTIVE: The student will demonstrate that he has developed his own criteria for critical review of (1) fiction, (b) propaganda, (c) nonfiction, (d) essays, (e) journals, and (f) biographies.

DIRECTIONS In the left column below are six different kinds of reading materials which a student should be able to review critically. In the right column are some criteria for evaluating these materials. Match appropriate criteria to the types of materials by writing the number of the criteria in the space beneath the specific material. Some criteria are appropriate for more than one material. You may list other criteria.

Reading Materials

a. Fiction

 __1__   __6__   __7__   __14__

 Other _____

b. Propaganda

 __1__   __2__   __11__   __12__

 Other _____

c. Nonfiction

 __3__   __4__   __6__   __12__

 Other _____

d. Essays

 __1__   __6__   __7__   __15__

 Other _____

e. Journals

 __4__   __17__   __18__   __19__

f. Biographies

 __1__   __6__   __9__   __10__

 Other _____

Criteria for Critical Review

1. Interesting
2. Subtle
3. Contains helpful information
4. Author is qualified to write book or article
5. Realistic to life
6. Ideas flow well
7. Entertaining
8. Exciting
9. Either entertaining or contains a message or moral
10. Accurate
11. Gets message across
12. There is a purpose behind the message
13. Can detect attitude of writer
14. Is written on level of the intended audience
15. Sticks closely to theme
16. Expresses thoughts concisely
17. Articles are in keeping with purposes of publication
18. Articles are well written
19. Attractive or practical layout
20. Content of articles valuable

MASTERY REQUIREMENT: Teacher judgment

Indicate mastery on the student response sheet with a check.

II. **COMPREHENSION**

Name _____

E. **Critical Evaluation**

Date _____

1. **Develops own criteria for critical review of materials:**

Mastery
a. _____
b. _____
c. _____
d. _____
e. _____
f. _____

a. **fiction**
b. **propaganda**
c. **nonfiction**
d. **essays**
e. **journals**
f. **biographies**

DIRECTIONS   In the left column below are six different kinds of reading materials which a student should be able to review critically. In the right column are some criteria for evaluating these materials. Match appropriate criteria to the types of materials by writing the number of the criteria in the space beneath the specific material. Some criteria are appropriate for more than one material. You may list other criteria.

Reading Materials

a. Fiction

____   ____   ____   ____

Other _____

b. Propaganda

____   ____   ____   ____

Other _____

c. Nonfiction

____   ____   ____   ____

Other _____

d. Essays

____   ____   ____   ____

Other _____

e. Journals

____   ____   ____   ____

f. Biographies

____   ____   ____   ____

Other _____

Criteria for Critical Review

1. Interesting
2. Subtle
3. Contains helpful information
4. Author is qualified to write book or article
5. Realistic to life
6. Ideas flow well
7. Entertaining
8. Exciting
9. Either entertaining or contains a message or moral
10. Accurate
11. Gets message across
12. There is a purpose behind the message
13. Can detect attitude of writer
14. Is written on level of the intended audience
15. Sticks closely to theme
16. Expresses thoughts concisely
17. Articles are in keeping with purposes of publication
18. Articles are well written
19. Attractive or practical layout
20. Content of articles valuable

II. COMPREHENSION   E. Critical Evaluation   2. **Makes judgments about the author's qualifications**

OBJECTIVE: The student will make judgments about the author's qualifications.

DIRECTIONS: Read the following items. From the information provided make a judgment about the author's qualification for the work indicated. If you think the author is qualified, write "1" in the space provided. If he or she does not seem qualified, write "2."

  2   1. Pete Star, an outstanding hitter for the Cincinnati Reds, has just published a scientific treatise pertaining to the lunar effects on tides.

  1   2. Gil Johnson, a traveling salesman, is the author of a best selling novel.

  1   3. A school principal wrote an article for *Business Week* on girls in scholastic programs.

  2   4. The Senator from Montana recently published a feature article on makeup tips for teenage girls.

  2   5. The headline in tonight's paper was "The Effects of Marijuana on Teenage Youth." The article was written by Mrs. Susan Crabtree, a housewife.

  1   6. R. B. Smith, author of several novels, was the luncheon speaker. His address was entitled "Writing as an Avocation."

  1   7. The minister wrote a book of prayers.

  1   8. This month's book review focused on reading hints for young children. It was written by the noted educator and author Marguerite Bishop.

  2   9. The vegetarian, Buster Stone, is being considered for an award for the publication "100 Different Ways of Cooking Beef."

  2   10. Chris Edwards, winner of many national and international tennis meets, has submitted a manuscript on the "Alternatives to International Affairs."

MASTERY REQUIREMENT: 8 correct responses

Indicate mastery on the student response sheet with a check.

ADVANCED LEVEL—Part Two

II. COMPREHENSION

Name _____

E. Critical Evaluation

Date _____

2. **Makes judgments about the author's qualifications**

Mastery _____

DIRECTIONS: Read the following items. From the information provided make a judgment about the author's qualification for the work indicated. If you think the author is qualified, write "1" in the space provided. If he or she does not seem qualified, write "2."

_____ 1. Pete Star, an outstanding hitter for the Cincinnati Reds, has just published a scientific treatise pertaining to the lunar effects on tides.

_____ 2. Gil Johnson, a traveling salesman, is the author of a best selling novel.

_____ 3. A school principal wrote an article for *Business Week* on girls in scholastic programs.

_____ 4. The Senator from Montana recently published a feature article on makeup tips for teenage girls.

_____ 5. The headline in tonight's paper was "The Effects of Marijuana on Teenage Youth." The article was written by Mrs. Susan Crabtree, a housewife.

_____ 6. R. B. Smith, author of several novels, was the luncheon speaker. His address was entitled "Writing as an Avocation."

_____ 7. The minister wrote a book of prayers.

_____ 8. This month's book review focused on reading hints for young children. It was written by the noted educator and author Marguerite Bishop.

_____ 9. The vegetarian, Buster Stone, is being considered for an award for the publication "100 Different Ways of Cooking Beef."

_____ 10. Chris Edwards, winner of many national and international tennis meets, has submitted a manuscript on the "Alternatives to International Affairs."

II.   COMPREHENSION   E.   Critical Evaluation   3.   Judges reasonableness between
                                                              statements and conclusions

OBJECTIVE: The student will judge the reasonableness between statements and conclusions.

DIRECTIONS: Decide if the following conclusions are true or false, based upon the informa-
                tion given. Write the letter "T" beside each conclusion which you consider to
                be true and an "F" by each one that is false.

__T__   1.   A person can become well-informed by reading widely.

__F__   2.   The sun is shining; therefore, it can not possibly rain today.

__F__   3.   All rich people are dishonest.

__T__   4.   C is larger than A but smaller than B; therefore, A is smaller than either B or C.

__F__   5.   A person who reads a lot is well-informed.

__F__   6.   A thesaurus is better than a dictionary.

__T__   7.   A is to B as B is to C; therefore, B has the same relationship to A as to C.

__F__   8.   Carl, our brightest student, is small and poorly coordinated. Very bright people are
             seldom good athletes.

MASTERY REQUIREMENT: 6 correct responses

Indicate mastery on the student response sheet with a check.

ADVANCED LEVEL—Part Two

II. COMPREHENSION

Name _____

    E. Critical Evaluation

Date _____

       3. Judges reasonableness between
          statements and conclusions

Mastery _____

DIRECTIONS: Decide if the following conclusions are true or false, based upon the information given. Write the letter "T" beside each conclusion which you consider to be true and an "F" by each one that is false.

_____ 1. A person can become well-informed by reading widely.

_____ 2. The sun is shining; therefore, it can not possibly rain today.

_____ 3. All rich people are dishonest.

_____ 4. C is larger than A but smaller than B; therefore, A is smaller than either B or C.

_____ 5. A person who reads a lot is well-informed.

_____ 6. A thesaurus is better than a dictionary.

_____ 7. A is to B as B is to C; therefore, B has the same relationship to A as to C.

_____ 8. Carl, our brightest student, is small and poorly coordinated. Very bright people are seldom good athletes.

III.   STUDY SKILLS   A.   Uses Thesaurus, Almanac, Atlas, Maps and Globes

OBJECTIVE: The student will demonstrate that he/she can use the thesaurus, almanac, atlas, maps, and globes.

DIRECTIONS: Indicate the reference tool you would use to find the information below. Write the appropriate number in the space provided.

1. Thesaurus   2. Almanac   3. Atlas   4. Map   5. Globe

___1___   1. Synonyms

___3___   2. Square miles of Japan

___4___   3. The shortest route to the capitol of your state

___2___   4. The baseball player who hit the most runs during 1975

___3___   5. The altitude of Mt. Everest

___5___   6. The geographic location of Spain in relation to the United States

___1___   7. Another word to use that means the same as "incline"

___2___   8. When the next full moon will occur

3 / 4 / 5   9. The locations of the Great Lakes

___5___   10. Continents located above and below the equator

MASTERY REQUIREMENT: 8 correct responses

Indicate mastery on the student response sheet with a check.

ADVANCED LEVEL—Part Two

III. STUDY SKILLS

Name _____

A. Uses Thesaurus, Almanac,
Atlas, Maps and Globes

Date _____

Mastery _____

DIRECTIONS: Indicate the reference tool you would use to find the information below. Write the appropriate number in the space provided.

1. Thesaurus   2. Almanac   3. Atlas   4. Map   5. Globe

_____   1. Synonyms

_____   2. Square miles of Japan

_____   3. The shortest route to the capitol of your state

_____   4. The baseball player who hit the most runs during 1975

_____   5. The altitude of Mt. Everest

_____   6. The geographic location of Spain in relation to the United States

_____   7. Another word to use that means the same as "incline"

_____   8. When the next full moon will occur

_____   9. The locations of the Great Lakes

_____   10. Continents located above and below the equator

III.   STUDY SKILLS   B.   Uses Variety of Media to Complete Assignments and Purposes

OBJECTIVE: The student will demonstrate that he/she uses a variety of media to complete assignments and purposes.

DIRECTIONS: Make assignments that require the use of various media to complete properly. Observe the student over a period of a few days or a few weeks. Check the media used in completing recent assignments.

_____   dictionary

_____   thesaurus

_____   card catalog

_____   atlas

_____   maps

_____   globes

_____   newspapers

_____   magazines

_____   almanac

_____   textbook

_____   filmstrips

_____   resource people (including teacher)

MASTERY REQUIREMENT: Teacher judgment

Indicate mastery on the student response sheet with a check.

ADVANCED LEVEL—Part Two

III. STUDY SKILLS

    B. Uses Variety of Media to
        Complete Assignments and
        Purposes

Name _____

Date _____

Mastery _____

DIRECTIONS: Check the media used in completing recent assignments.

_____ dictionary

_____ thesaurus

_____ card catalog

_____ atlas

_____ maps

_____ globes

_____ newspapers

_____ magazines

_____ almanac

_____ textbook

_____ filmstrips

_____ resource people (including teacher)

III.   STUDY SKILLS   C.   1.   Uses Outlining Skills

OBJECTIVE: The student will use outlining skills.

DIRECTIONS: Read the following information, then prepare a simple outline of the material in the space provided.

As the population of the world increases there is an ever increasing demand for raw materials. Coal, gas, and oil are needed for fuels. Iron, copper, and aluminum ores are needed for refining into metals. This increase in demand for raw materials has led to expanded exploration for minerals on land and beneath the seas.

People go to bed hungry each night in many parts of the world. Because of the food shortage, efforts are being made to increase production through soil conservation, use of fertilizers, and through crop rotation. In searching for additional sources of food, we are now studying the sea and air more closely.

OUTLINE: (Should be similar to outline below)

I.   Demand for raw materials

    A.   Fuel
        1.   Coal
        2.   Gas
        3.   Oil
    B.   Metals
        1.   Iron
        2.   Copper
        3.   Aluminum

II.   Food shortage

    A.   Increase production
        1.   Soil conservation
        2.   Use of fertilizers
        3.   Crop rotation
    B.   Search for other sources
        1.   Air
        2.   Sea

MASTERY REQUIREMENT: Teacher judgment

Indicate mastery on the student response sheet wth a check.

ADVANCED LEVEL—Part Two

III. STUDY SKILLS

    C. 1. Uses Outlining Skills

Name _____

Date _____

Mastery _____

DIRECTIONS: Read the following information, then prepare a simple outline of the material in the space provided.

As the population of the world increases there is an ever increasing demand for raw materials. Coal, gas, and oil are needed for fuels. Iron, copper, and aluminum ores are needed for refining into metals. This increase in demand for raw materials has led to expanded exploration for minerals on land and beneath the seas.

People go to bed hungry each night in many parts of the world. Because of the food shortage, efforts are being made to increase production through soil conservation, use of fertilizers, and through crop rotation. In searching for additional sources of food, we are now studying the sea and air more closely.

OUTLINE:

I.

    A.

        1.

        2.

        3.

    B.

        1.

        2.

        3.

II.

    A.

        1.

        2.

        3.

    B.

        1.

        2.

III. STUDY SKILLS   C. 2.   Uses Note-taking Skills

OBJECTIVE: The student will use note-taking skills.

DIRECTIONS: Study the following passage and take notes so that you can answer questions if called upon to do so.

During the late 1940's and the early 1950's when nuclear energy was mentioned, almost everyone thought of atomic bombs. Today, the concept of nuclear energy is quite different. We now have huge power plants that change nuclear energy into electrical energy. Aircraft carriers and submarines also operate on nuclear energy.

Nuclear energy is produced when the nucleus of an atom is changed. The first nuclear reactions took place naturally. In natural nuclear reactions, some elements break up by themselves. When this occurs, new elements are formed and energy is released. Elements that change through the alteration of the nucleus are called radioactive elements. It took scientists many years to understand these reactions and to bring them under control.

NOTES: (must cover major points, similar to those below)

Nuclear energy

   —associated with atomic bomb in 40's and 50's

   —now runs power plants, ships, etc.

   —nucleus of atom changes—produces energy

   —nuclear change occurs naturally in radioactive elements

   —scientists can now control this change

MASTERY REQUIREMENT: Teacher judgment

Indicate mastery on the student response sheet with a check.

ADVANCED LEVEL—Part Two

III.   STUDY SKILLS

Name _____

C. 2.   Uses Note-taking
         Skills

Date _____

Mastery _____

DIRECTIONS: Study the following passage and take notes so that you can answer questions if called upon to do so.

During the late 1940's and the early 1950's when nuclear energy was mentioned, almost everyone thought of atomic bombs. Today, the concept of nuclear energy is quite different. We now have huge power plants that change nuclear energy into electrical energy. Aircraft carriers and submarines also operate on nuclear energy.

Nuclear energy is produced when the nucleus of an atom is changed. The first nuclear reactions took place naturally. In natural nuclear reactions, some elements break up by themselves. When this occurs, new elements are formed and energy is released. Elements that change through the alteration of the nucleus are called radioactive elements. It took scientists many years to understand these reactions and to bring them under control.

NOTES:

III.   STUDY SKILLS   D.   Adjusts Reading Speed to Material and Purpose
                      E.   Demonstrates Independence in Locating, Selecting and Using
                           Materials to Own Purpose
                      F.   Applies Problem Solving Approach: Identifies Problem, Gathers
                           Information, Devises Possible Solution, Selects Options,
                           Evaluates
                      G.   Designs, Uses and Revises Own Study Schedules

OBJECTIVE: The student will demonstrate that he uses study skills effectively.

DIRECTIONS: Observe the student over a period of several days or weeks. Set up situations
              in class and make assignments that encourage the use of the study skills listed
              above.

Observation Check List

D

_____   1.   Scans material hurriedly to get content
_____   2.   Skims to find appropriate material or to locate specific information
_____   3.   Reads technical materials carefully
_____   4.   Reads easy materials rapidly

E

_____   5.   Can locate specific information and answers to questions rapidly
_____   6.   Needs little direction in locating and selecting appropriate materials

F

_____   7.   Knows how to logically go about solving problems
_____   8.   Thoroughly understands problem before attempting solution
_____   9.   Attempts to gather sufficient data on question at hand
_____   10. Can offer alternative solutions
_____   11. Seldom jumps to conclusions

G

_____   12. Uses study time wisely
_____   13. Does not require prodding
_____   14. Completes long assignments as well as short ones

MASTERY REQUIREMENT: Teacher judgment

Indicate mastery on the student response sheet with a check.

III. STUDY SKILLS

Name _____

D. Adjusts Reading Speed to
   Material and Purpose
E. Demonstrates Independence
   in Locating, Selecting and
   Using Materials to Own
   Purpose
F. Applies Problem Solving
   Approach: Identifies
   Problem, Gathers
   Information, Devises
   Possible Solution, Selects
   Options, Evaluates
G. Designs, Uses and Revises
   Own Study Schedules

Date _____

Mastery:
   D. Adjusts Speed _____
   E. Locating, Selecting,
      Using Materials _____
   F. Problem Solving _____
   G. Study Schedules _____

DIRECTIONS: Observe the student over a period of several days or weeks. Set up situations in class and make assignments that encourage the use of the study skills listed above.

Observation Check List

D

1. Scans material hurriedly to get content
2. Skims to find appropriate material or to locate specific information
3. Reads technical materials carefully
4. Reads easy materials rapidly

E

5. Can locate specific information and answers to questions rapidly
6. Needs little direction in locating and selecting appropriate materials

F

7. Knows how to logically go about solving problems
8. Thoroughly understands problem before attempting solution
9. Attempts to gather sufficient data on question at hand
10. Can offer alternative solutions
11. Seldom jumps to conclusions

G

12. Uses study time wisely
13. Does not require prodding
14. Completes long assignments as well as short ones

III.   STUDY SKILLS   H.   Locates Sources within a Book by Using Table of Contents and
                                        Index

OBJECTIVE: The student will demonstrate that he/she can locate sources within a book by using
                      the table of contents and the index.

DIRECTIONS: Study the "Table of Contents" and the "Index" below. Then answer the ques-
                      tions that follow.

CONTENTS

INDEX

_27_   1.   On what page would you find a test for an adjective?

_3_   2.   Which chapter deals primarily with writing?

_29_   3.   On what page can you find information about "where" used as an adverb?

_2_   4.   In which chapter is information about "where" used as an adverb found?

Index   5.   Which gives the more specific location information, the table of contents or the
              index?

Table of
Contents 6.   Which shows how the book is organized?

Table of
Contents 7.   If you wanted to know the general contents of a chapter, which would you study,
              the table of contents or the index?

Pg. 300   8.   Where would you find information about acronyms?

Index   9.   In which is alphabetical order important, table of contents or index?

Index   10.   If you wanted to find information about adjectives quickly, where would you look?

MASTERY REQUIREMENT: 9 correct responses

Indicate mastery on the student response sheet with a check.

ADVANCED LEVEL—Part Two

III. STUDY SKILLS

H. Locates Sources within
     a Book by Using Table
     of Contents and Index

Name _____

Date _____

Mastery _____

DIRECTIONS: Study the "Table of Contents" and the "Index" below. Then answer the questions that follow.

_____ 1. On what page would you find a test for an adjective?

_____ 2. Which chapter deals primarily with writing?

_____ 3. On what page can you find information about "where" used as an adverb?

_____ 4. In which chapter is information about "where" used as an adverb found?

_____ 5. Which gives the more specific location information, the table of contents or the index?

_____ 6. Which shows how the book is organized?

_____ 7. If you wanted to know the general contents of a chapter, which would you study, the table of contents or the index?

_____ 8. Where would you find information about acronyms?

_____ 9. In which is alphabetical order important, table of contents or index?

_____ 10. If you wanted to find information about adjectives quickly, where would you look?

IV. CREATIVE READING   A. Recognizes Figurative Language, Dialect, and
                                Colloquial Speech

OBJECTIVE: The student will demonstrate that he or she recognizes figurative language, dialect and colloquial speech.

DIRECTIONS: Classify the following statements as (a) figurative language, (b) dialect, or (c) colloquial speech by placing the appropriate letter in the space provided before each statement.

    a. figurative language
    b. dialect
    c. colloquial speech

  __a__   1. She looked as fresh as the dew on a rose.

  __b__   2. This old house ain't much no more.

  __b__   3. Bill is fixin' to ride the critter.

  __c__   4. That there barn needs to be painted.

  __a__   5. She has been walking on air since her engagement.

  __c__   6. The stallion was chomping at the bits.

  __a__   7. The little boy was as quiet as a mouse.

  __b__   8. "He has a good idear."

  __c__   9. I've got it.

  __b__   10. "Dat pie sho wuz good, Miz Jones."

MASTERY REQUIREMENT: 7 correct responses

Indicate mastery on the student response sheet with a check.

ADVANCED LEVEL—Part Two

IV. CREATIVE READING

Name _____

A. Recognizes Figurative
Language, Dialect,
and Colloquial Speech

Date _____

Mastery _____

DIRECTIONS: Classify the following statements as (a) figurative language, (b) dialect, or (c) colloquial speech by placing the appropriate letter in the space provided before each statement.

a. figurative language
b. dialect
c. colloquial speech

_____ 1. She looked as fresh as the dew on a rose.

_____ 2. This old house ain't much no more.

_____ 3. Bill is fixin' to ride the critter.

_____ 4. That there barn needs to be painted.

_____ 5. She has been walking on air since her engagement.

_____ 6. The stallion was chomping at the bits.

_____ 7. The little boy was as quiet as a mouse.

_____ 8. "He has a good idear."

_____ 9. I've got it.

_____ 10. "Dat pie sho wuz good, Miz Jones."

IV. CREATIVE READING   B. Understands Literary Forms   1. Folk literature: tales, songs, fables, legends, and myths

OBJECTIVE: The student will demonstrate that he/she understands the different types of folk literature.

DIRECTIONS: Classify each of the following selections as either a (a) tale, (b) song, (c) fable, (d) legend, or (e) myth by placing the appropriate letter in the space provided before each selection.

    a. tale
    b. song
    c. fable
    d. legend
    e. myth

__c__ 1. The fox said, "The grapes were probably sour anyway."

__a__ 2. Two mosquitoes came into the room. One sat on the head of the bed and the other at the foot. "Shall we eat him here or take him outside," said the one at the head. "Let's eat him here. If we take him outside the big ones will get him," replied the other mosquito.

__b__ 3. I'll sing you a song about my mountain home.

__c__ 4. And men still swear that they have seen Big Foot high up in the mountains.

__d__ 5. Daniel Boone could track Indians better than most bloodhounds.

MASTERY REQUIREMENT: 5 correct responses

Indicate mastery on the student response sheet with a check.

ADVANCED LEVEL–Part Two

IV. CREATIVE READING

Name _____

B. Understands Literary
   Forms

Date _____

1. Folk literature: tales,
   songs, fables, legends,
   and myths

Mastery _____

DIRECTIONS: Classify each of the following selections as either a (a) tale, (b) song, (c) fable, (d) legend, or (e) myth by placing the appropriate letter in the space provided before each selection.·

   a. tale
   b. song
   c. fable
   d. legend
   e. myth

_____ 1. The fox said, "The grapes were probably sour anyway."

_____ 2. Two mosquitoes came into the room. One sat on the head of the bed and the other at the foot. "Shall we eat him here or take him outside," said the one at the head. "Let's eat him here. If we take him outside the big ones will get him," replied the other mosquito.

_____ 3. I'll sing you a song about my mountain home.

_____ 4. And men still swear that they have seen Big Foot high up in the mountains.

_____ 5. Daniel Boone could track Indians better than most bloodhounds.

IV. CREATIVE READING   B. Understands Literary Forms   2. Short Story
                                                            3. Nonfiction, includ-
                                                                ing propaganda
                                                            4. Poetry, limerick,
                                                                couplet, sonnet,
                                                                blank verse, and
                                                                internal rhyme

OBJECTIVE: The student will demonstrate that he/she understands literary forms such as the short story, nonfiction including propaganda, poetry, limerick, couplet, sonnet, blank verse and internal rhyme.

DIRECTIONS: Below are definitions of nine literary forms. Match each literary form to the correct definition by placing the appropriate letter in the space provided by the definitions.

a. short story   b. nonfiction   c. propaganda
d. poetry   e. limerick   f. couplet
g. sonnet   h. blank verse   i. internal rhyme

_h_   1. Unrhymed verse

_i_   2. Rhyme between a word within a line and another either at the end of the same line or within another line

_a_   3. An invented narrative with a full plot, but much shorter than a novel

_c_   4. Systematic efforts to spread opinions or beliefs

_b_   5. Prose literature that is not a novel, short story, or other form of writing based on imaginary people and events

_d_   6. Composition in verse showing great beauty or nobility of language arranged to create a specific emotional response through meaning, sound, and rhythm

_e_   7. A light or humorous verse of five lines of which lines 1, 2, and 5 are of three feet and lines 3 and 4 are of two feet with a rhyme scheme of a a b b a.

_g_   8. A poem having fourteen lines, typically of five-foot iambics rhyming according to a certain scheme.

_f_   9. Two successive lines of poetry, especially two that rhyme and are equally long.

MASTERY REQUIREMENT: 7 correct responses

Indicate mastery on the student response sheet with a check.

ADVANCED LEVEL—Part Two

IV. CREATIVE READING

Name _____

B. Understands Literary Forms

2. Short Story
3. Nonfiction, including propaganda
4. Poetry, limerick, couplet, sonnet, blank verse, and internal rhyme

Date _____

Mastery _____

DIRECTIONS: Below are definitions of nine literary forms. Match each literary form to the correct definition by placing the appropriate letter in the space provided by the definitions.

a. short story	b. nonfiction	c. propaganda
d. poetry	e. limerick	f. couplet
g. sonnet	h. blank verse	i. internal rhyme

_____ 1. Unrhymed verse

_____ 2. Rhyme between a word within a line and another either at the end of the same line or within another line

_____ 3. An invented narrative with a full plot, but much shorter than a novel

_____ 4. Systematic efforts to spread opinions or beliefs

_____ 5. Prose literature that is not a novel, short story, or other form of writing based on imaginary people and events

_____ 6. Composition in verse showing great beauty or nobility of language arranged to create a specific emotional response through meaning, sound, and rhythm

_____ 7. A light or humorous verse of five lines of which lines 1, 2, and 5 are of three feet and lines 3 and 4 are of two feet with a rhyme scheme of a a b b a.

_____ 8. A poem having fourteen lines, typically of five-foot iambics rhyming according to a certain scheme.

_____ 9. Two successive lines of poetry, especially two that rhyme and are equally long.

IV. CREATIVE READING   C. Compares Value Systems of Characters

OBJECTIVE: The student will demonstrate ability to compare value systems of characters.

DIRECTIONS: Read the following passage, then place a "D" by each word that reflects the value system of Dale. Place a "J" by each word that reflects the value system of Jim.

"What's wrong with making A's?" said Jim.

"Nothing if you want to be a bookworm. You know, some people just don't care about being sociable," said Dale. "Me, I'd rather use my time having a little fun. My girlfriend will feed me enough information during exams to get me by."

"I believe a person should develop good work habits in school. They will come in handy throughout life," Jim said as he walked away.

J	1.	foresight	D	7.	dishonest
D	2.	carefree	J	8.	trustworthy
D	3.	unconcerned	J	9.	thoughtful
J	4.	honest	D	10.	opinionated
J	5.	caring	J and D	11.	sincere
J	6.	good worker	J and D	12.	truthful

MASTERY REQUIREMENT: 10 correct responses

Indicate mastery on the student response sheet with a check.

IV. CREATIVE READING

C. Compares Value
Systems of
Characters

Name _____

Date _____

Mastery _____

DIRECTIONS: Read the following passage, then place a "D" by each word that reflects the value system of Dale. Place a "J" by each word that reflects the value system of Jim.

"What's wrong with making A's?" said Jim.

"Nothing if you want to be a bookworm. You know, some people just don't care about being sociable," said Dale. "Me, I'd rather use my time having a little fun. My girlfriend will feed me enough information during exams to get me by."

"I believe a person should develop good work habits in school. They will come in handy throughout life," Jim said as he walked away.

_____	1. foresight		_____	7. dishonest
_____	2. carefree		_____	8. trustworthy
_____	3. unconcerned		_____	9. thoughtful
_____	4. honest		_____	10. opinionated
_____	5. caring		_____	11. sincere
_____	6. good worker		_____	12. truthful

IV. CREATIVE READING   D. Understands Settings: Social, Economic, and Educational

OBJECTIVE: The student will demonstrate that he/she understands social settings.

DIRECTIONS: Read the following statements carefully. Classify each setting as social, economic, or educational by writing the appropriate letter in the space before each statement.

     a. social   b. economic   c. educational

__a__ 1. The well-trimmed lawn was decorated with gaily colored umbrellas.

__c__ 2. Inside the ivy covered walls of the classroom is where one is often prepared to cope with the real problems of life.

__b__ 3. The bank president coughed lightly, indicating that he was ready to see his next customer.

__c__ 4. The numerous bowed heads around the library table told observers that exam time was near.

__b__ 5. The cigar smoke hung lifelessly above the stockbroker's desk.

__a__ 6. The large sterling punch bowl dominated the food laden table.

MASTERY REQUIREMENT: All correct

Indicate mastery on the student response sheet with a check.

ADVANCED LEVEL—Part Two

IV. CREATIVE READING   Name _____

     D. Understands Settings:
         Social, Economic, and   Date _____
         Educational

                                        Mastery _____

DIRECTIONS: Read the following statements carefully. Classify each setting as social, eco-
             nomic, or educational by writing the appropriate letter in the space before
             each statement.

         a. social   b. economic   c. educational

_____ 1. The well-trimmed lawn was decorated with gaily colored umbrellas.

_____ 2. Inside the ivy covered walls of the classroom is where one is often prepared to cope
            with the real problems of life.

_____ 3. The bank president coughed lightly, indicating that he was ready to see his next
            customer.

_____ 4. The numerous bowed heads around the library table told observers that exam time
            was near.

_____ 5. The cigar smoke hung lifelessly above the stockbroker's desk.

_____ 6. The large sterling punch bowl dominated the food laden table.

IV.   CREATIVE READING   E.   Responds to Author's Background

OBJECTIVE: The student will respond to the author's background.

DIRECTIONS: Read the following passage. Place a check (√) beside each word or phrase that describes the author's background.

Her fingers bled sparingly around the nails as if she had been picking cotton for a week. As she placed her hands into the water, the sting made her withdraw them quickly. This experience took her back to the days when, during the fall season, she was in the cotton fields snatching locks of white fluff while the early morning dew bit the raw open breaks in her skin. Those early memories she could do without.

The author's writing reveals that he grew up:

_____   1.   in the city

_____   2.   in the wheat country of the Midwestern plains

__√__   3.   in the South

__√__   4.   before 1965

__√__   5.   on a farm

_____   6.   the son of a wealthy plantation owner

MASTERY REQUIREMENT: 5 correct responses

Indicate mastery on the student response sheet with a check.

ADVANCED LEVEL—Part Two

IV. CREATIVE READING

Name _____

E. Responds to Author's
Background

Date _____

Mastery _____

DIRECTIONS: Read the following passage. Place a check (√) beside each word or phrase that describes the author's background.

Her fingers bled sparingly around the nails as if she had been picking cotton for a week. As she placed her hands into the water, the sting made her withdraw them quickly. This experience took her back to the days when, during the fall season, she was in the cotton fields snatching locks of white fluff while the early morning dew bit the raw open breaks in her skin. Those early memories she could do without.

The author's writing reveals that he grew up:

_____ 1. in the city

_____ 2. in the wheat country of the Midwestern plains

_____ 3. in the South

_____ 4. before 1965

_____ 5. on a farm

_____ 6. the son of a wealthy plantation owner

IV. CREATIVE READING   F.   Responds to the Author's Style of Mood and Point-Of-View

OBJECTIVE: The student will demonstrate that he/she respond to the author's style of mood and point-of-view.

DIRECTIONS: Read each of the following statements carefully, then indicate the <u>author's mood</u> by writing the appropriate letter in the space beside each <u>odd number</u>. Indicate the <u>author's point-of-view</u> by writing the appropriate letter beside each <u>even number</u>.

Mood	*Point-of-View*
a. fearful	a. friendship can be silent
b. rebellious	b. ecological concern
c. tender	c. conservative
d. hostile	d. willing to defend
e. sentimental	e. kindnesses are remembered

__b__ 1. "Down with taxes! The government is involved in too much wasteful spending."

__c__ 2.

__c/e__ 3. One seldom remembers the great events which alter the course of history, but the little things such as the smell of a rose on a dewy spring morning, the touch of a

__e__ 4. gentle hand, or a kind word spoken by a dear friend are never forgotten.

__a__ 5. Nuclear reactor plants are the most damnable curse of the century. They are the offsprings of warped, inebriated minds and will result in disaster for this and future

__b__ 6. generations.

__d__ 7. "I am ready to fight, and the first encroachment will bring bloodshed."

__d__ 8.

__c/e__ 9. "These are the moments to cherish—moments when two people sit quietly together

__a__ 10. —moments when one feels the true meaning of friendship."

MASTERY REQUIREMENT: 8 correct responses

Indicate mastery on the student response sheet with a check.

IV.   CREATIVE READING

Name _____

F.   Responds to the Author's
Style of Mood and Point-
of-View

Date _____

Mastery _____

DIRECTIONS: Read each of the following statements carefully, then indicate the author's mood by writing the appropriate letter in the space beside each odd number. Indicate the author's point-of-view by writing the appropriate letter beside each even number.

Mood	*Point of View*
a. fearful	a. friendship can be silent
b. rebellious	b. ecological concern
c. tender	c. conservative
d. hostile	d. willing to defend
e. sentimental	e. kindnesses are remembered

_____   1.   "Down with taxes! The government is involved in too much wasteful spending."
_____   2.

_____   3.   One seldom remembers the great events which alter the course of history, but the little things such as the smell of a rose on a dewy spring morning, the touch of a
_____   4.   gentle hand, or a kind word spoken by a dear friend are never forgotten.

_____   5.   Nuclear reactor plants are the most damnable curse of the century. They are the offsprings of warped, inebriated minds and will result in disaster for this and future
_____   6.   generations.

_____   7.   "I am ready to fight, and the first encroachment will bring bloodshed."
_____   8.

_____   9.   "These are the moments to cherish—moments when two people sit quietly together
_____ 10.   —moments when one feels the true meaning of friendship."

Name of Teacher: _____

GROUP SUMMARY

PROFILE

ADVANCED LEVEL

Student Names

I. Vocabulary:
A. Word Recognition in Content
B. Identifies Compound Words
C. Root Words
  1. Recognizes and understands concept of root words
  2. Knows meaning of common roots
D. Prefixes
  1. Recognizes and knows concept of prefixes
  2. Knows meaning of common prefixes:
E. Suffixes
  1. Recognizes and knows concept of suffixes
  2. Knows meaning of common suffixes
F. Knows meaning of terms in vocabulary
  1. simile   metaphor
  2. synonyms antonyms homonyms
  3. onomatopoeia
II. Word Attack Skills:
A. Knows consonant sounds
  1. Initial single consonants of one sound
  2. Sounds of c and **g**
  3. Blends digraph diphthong
  4. Medial sounds
  5. Final sounds
B. Hears and can make vowel sounds
  1. Long vowels short vowels
  2. Can apply vowel rules
C. Knows elements of syllabication
  1. Knows rules
  2. Can apply rules
D. Uses accent properly

PART ONE

1. Knows and applies rules
2. Can shift accent and change use of word

III. Comprehension:

A. Understands structure of story or paragraph

   main idea

   topic sentence

   sequence of ideas

   subordinate ideas

B. Can repeat general idea of material read

C. Can remember specific important facts

D. Can relate material read to known information

E. Can follow printed directions

F. Can interpret hidden meaning

IV. Silent and Oral Reading:

A. Reads silently without lip movements

B. Reads silently at twice oral rate

C. Adjusts silent rate to material

1. Reads popular fiction at 200+ words per minute
2. Uses skimming techniques when applicable

D. Eye-voice span 3 to 5 words (in oral reading)

E. Reads aloud with comprehension

I. Vocabulary:

A. Increases vocabulary through wide reading

B. Organizes own word study techniques

II. Comprehension:

A. Interpretation

1. Sequences events from multiple sources
2. Makes generalizations from multiple sources
3. Identifies relationships of elements from multiple sources
4. Identifies author's purpose
5. Develops use of parts of speech

B. Application

1. Uses multiple sources for documentation
2. Uses maps, graphs, charts, tables
3. Takes notes to summarize and respond
4. Uses reading for different purposes

PART TWO

Student Names

Column headings:

C. **Analysis**
1. Differentiates between types of sentences
D. **Synthesis**
1. Extends generalizations beyond sources
2. Hypothesizes
3. Suggests alternatives and options
E. **Critical Evaluation**
1. Develops own criteria for critical review
2. Makes judgments about author's qualifications
3. Judges reasonableness between statements and conclusions
III. **Study Skills:**
A. Uses thesaurus, almanac, atlas, maps and globes
B. Uses variety of media
C. Uses outlining and note-taking skills
D. Adjusts reading speed to material and purpose
E. Demonstrates independence in locating, selecting and using materials to own purpose
F. Applies problem solving approach
G. Designs, uses and revises own study schedules
H. Locates sources within a book
IV. **Creative Reading:**
A. Recognizes figurative language
B. Understands literary forms:
1. folk literature
2. short story
3. nonfiction including propaganda
4. poetry, limerick, couplet, sonnet, blank verse
C. Compares value systems of characters
D. Understands settings
E. Responds to the author's background
F. Responds to the author's style of mood and point-of-view

Name of Teacher: _____

GROUP SUMMARY
PROFILE
ADVANCED
LEVEL

Student Names

I. Vocabulary:		
A. Word Recognition in Content		
B. Identifies Compound Words		
C. Root Words		
1. Recognizes and understands concept of root words		
2. Knows meaning of common roots		
D. Prefixes		
1. Recognizes and knows concept of prefixes		
2. Knows meaning of common prefixes:		
E. Suffixes		
1. Recognizes and knows concept of suffixes		
2. Knows meaning of common suffixes		
F. Knows meaning of terms in vocabulary		
1. simile metaphor		
2. synonyms antonyms homonyms		
3. onomatopoeia		
II. Word Attack Skills:		
A. Knows consonant sounds		
1. Initial single consonants of one sound		
2. Sounds of c and g		
3. Blends digraph diphthong		
4. Medial sounds		
5. Final sounds		
B. Hears and can make vowel sounds		
1. Long vowels short vowels		
2. Can apply vowel rules		
C. Knows elements of syllabication		
1. Knows rules		
2. Can apply rules		
D. Uses accent properly		

PART ONE

1. Knows and applies rules
2. Can shift accent and change use of word

III. Comprehension:

A. Understands structure of story or paragraph
    main idea
    topic sentence
    sequence of ideas
    subordinate ideas

B. Can repeat general idea of material read
C. Can remember specific important facts
D. Can relate material read to known information
E. Can follow printed directions
F. Can interpret hidden meaning

IV. Silent and Oral Reading:

A. Reads silently without lip movements
B. Reads silently at twice oral rate
C. Adjusts silent rate to material
    1. Reads popular fiction at 200+ words per minute
    2. Uses skimming techniques when applicable
D. Eye-voice span 3 to 5 words (in oral reading)
E. Reads aloud with comprehension

I. Vocabulary:

A. Increases vocabulary through wide reading
B. Organizes own word study techniques

II. Comprehension:

A. Interpretation
    1. Sequences events from multiple sources
    2. Makes generalizations from multiple sources
    3. Identifies relationships of elements from multiple sources
    4. Identifies author's purpose
    5. Develops use of parts of speech

B. Application
    1. Uses multiple sources for documentation
    2. Uses maps, graphs, charts, tables
    3. Takes notes to summarize and respond
    4. Uses reading for different purposes

PART TWO

Student Names

C. Analysis
1. Differentiates between types of sentences
D. Synthesis
1. Extends generalizations beyond sources
2. Hypothesizes
3. Suggests alternatives and options
E. Critical Evaluation
1. Develops own criteria for critical review
2. Makes judgments about author's qualifications
3. Judges reasonableness between statements and conclusions

III. Study Skills:
A. Uses thesaurus, almanac, atlas, maps and globes
B. Uses variety of media
C. Uses outlining and note-taking skills
D. Adjusts reading speed to material and purpose
E. Demonstrates independence in locating, selecting and using materials to own purpose
F. Applies problem solving approach
G. Designs, uses and revises own study schedules
H. Locates sources within a book

IV. Creative Reading:
A. Recognizes figurative language
B. Understands literary forms:
1. folk literature
2. short story
3. nonfiction including propaganda
4. poetry, limerick, couplet, sonnet, blank verse
C. Compares value systems of characters
D. Understands settings
E. Responds to the author's background
F. Responds to the author's style of mood and point view